STILL STANDING

Michelle Harrell

Around HIM
PUBLISHING

0

Table of Contents

Introduction

What do you do when you've done all you can
And it seems like it's never enough?
And what do you say when your friends turn away
And you're all alone, alone?
Tell me what do you give when you've given your all
And it seems like you can't make it through?

Well you just stand when there's nothing left to do
You just stand; let the Lord see you through
Yes after you've done all you can, you just stand.

Tell me how do you handle the guilt of your past?
Tell me how do you deal with the shame?
And how can you smile when your heart has been broken
And filled with pain, filled with pain?
Tell me what do you give when you've given your all
Seems like you can't make it through?

Child you just stand when there's nothing left to do
You just stand, let the Lord see you through.
Yes after you've done all you can, you just stand.

Donnie McClurkin

Preface

First, I'm thankful to God for putting it in me to write this book. Secondly, I'm thankful for the experiences in this book. That sounds crazy, huh? No one would want to go through this. Trust me, I didn't either, but for the first time in my life I'm looking at the situation as a half full glass, not half empty. I liken this experience to Christ's journey. No, I'm nowhere close to being Christ, but let me make my point. Jesus went through a whole lot, even as a child, BUT God's intention was to get the glory from the salvation of His people. My journey was horrible, but in me sharing my story, someone will be blessed. Someone will stand up to their abuser and say "no more." Someone will be delivered from the burdens they carry from their own story. Someone will recognize that whatever they're going through is nothing God can't handle. Give it to HIM and wait. It will never be a delivery convenient for you, but as my Grandma used to say, "it will be on time". Sometimes we feel like God has abandoned us, but as with all good things, God's glory and deliverance is abundant. His grace is sufficient and He is there for us. This book will help someone get to their "aha" moment.

Now what this book is NOT meant to do is embarrass anyone, hurt anyone or put anyone's business on "blast". This book is part of my healing. Part of my "getting to the next phase". My own "aha" moment. I've been through so much in my life, but God has kept me. When I look at what and where I could have been, I'm truly thankful for where I am and more than excited about where I'm going. God has a plan for my life- this I know. I don't know what the complete plan is, but I know that I'm a tool. An instrument that He's using to help someone else. And in my helping someone else, not only will it be a blessing to me, but more importantly, God will get the glory out of it.

You see, my story, whether directly or indirectly, has affected so many people. My journey, my experience, my "theft of childhood", has torn up families, has had family members carrying animosity toward each other and has put people in the position of having to choose sides. God isn't happy with any of that, but He will get the glory out of it and He's doing so now.

Every time my pen hits the paper I know God is smiling. I feel His encouragement and for that I'm thankful.

Still Standing

In a nutshell, my story is one of a little girl being raped and molested by her step-father, shunned and outcast by her family, especially her mother and the re-count of the trials and tribulations afterward. Rape and molestation baggage doesn't go away when the abuse stops. Oh no, that's a myth. It's a lifelong scar that is not only on the body, but forever etched in one's heart.

That's where we, the victims, have to decide to become VICTORS. It's what we do, how we handle, what happened to us, that makes us VICTORS.

We'll use VICTORS as an acronym for V-victory, I-in, C-Christ, T-to, O-overcome, R-rape, S-scars. OOOhh, God just gave that to me. Thank you God! My whole being praises God for this and for having me share my story. NOW I WILL ADVISE YOU TO PRAY BEFORE YOU READ THIS. If you are a believer, stop right now and ask God for peace, understanding and wisdom when you read this. Peace to not lose sleep at night when you read some of these chapters, understanding so that hate and anger won't build up in your heart and wisdom to be able to receive the blessing from this. Not hold on to the negative, but receive only the positive. I am no longer a victim, but forever a VICTOR. And more importantly- I'M STILL STANDING.

Chapter 1: A Mother's Love?

In most cases, there is nothing more precious than a mother's love. Even though Dads play an important part in conception its all up to mom after that. Her daily activities, what she eats and drinks, whether she rests or not, they all affect the baby. I would dare say moms cherish pregnancy. We are the sole care givers for that time. Our babies get used to the sound of our voices, our daily routine and our heartbeat creating what should be a never ending bond.

As moms, we go through the tedious process of labor, but it produces this precious little person. One look and normally, the love we thought we felt during pregnancy increases 100,000 fold. Under normal circumstances the bond grows and its one of the best feelings a woman can have. In some cases, Mommy didn't give birth to the child, but is a Mommy just the same. The same love, sense of protection and bond is there.

Girls, more often than not, are die hard "Daddy's Girls". I know I am. But there's something special about Mommy, too. When we want to be loved and spoiled we turn to Daddy. But when we need nurturing, let us fall and get a boo-boo or someone hurts our feelings we call on Mommy.

I never got that from her. Her who? My egg-donor. What the heck is an egg-donor you say? Well, when a man fathers a child and has little to do with being a nurturing, caring, responsible dad we call him a "sperm donor".

Thus, the title "egg-donor" fits perfectly for my biological mother. Don't forget that term. I don't want you to get confused when I tell you about my mom. Ok? Ok!

I realized very early on I wasn't a priority to her. Not sure why, but I wasn't. Part of me feels like it's because I'm the BIGGEST DADDY'S GIRL IN THE WORLD!!! I was conceived when they were young and I think she was looking for a husband and at 19, marriage wasn't on his mind. So how dare I be a Daddy's girl! I think she took out on me her anger and resentment towards him. My grandma once told me she slapped me so hard when she was mad at him that it left her hand print on my face for a few days. That's one of the little secrets she (Grandma) and I shared. I don't remember it and I'm sure I wasn't supposed to know about it. I think because I'm so in love with my Daddy that it made me an easy target. I have a dent (more like a crater) in my head that's been there for as long as I can remember. I've always wondered if she threw me down some stairs or something like that because when I say it's big, it's BIG. It's just not normal for someone to have that kind of dent in their head. Unless my skull split open when I was born and had to be sewn back together I just don't understand how that dent got there. My cousin said I fell off the porch when I was in my walker, but he never mentioned hospitalization or anything like that so I don't think it came from that. I hope I never have to shave my head. It would NOT be cute at all!

When we were growing up, and by we, I mean my sister, cousins and myself, we always did things together. We took family trips and spent time together all the time. We were the ideal family for the most part. That is until my egg-donor married her current husband, i.e. my step-father, i.e. my abuser. Anyway, we went everywhere together and when I say we went on trips, everybody went. Grandma and Grandaddy, their children and all the grandchildren went on trips together. Kings Dominion, Bush Gardens, White Lake Beach, Little Washington Beach... we did it all. One day, my grandparents were taking the grandchildren to Little Washington Beach to eat fried crabs and to play in the water, but I gave some lame excuse why I didn't want to go. It wasn't that I didn't want to go and be with my cousins and sister, but I was hoping to spend some time with my egg-donor. Once the van (my granddaddy had one of those multi-passenger vans to transport all of us) pulled off I asked her to play hide and seek with me as we were still outside. She hid, I counted and went to find her. She wasn't in the yard and when I went to go look for her in the house the door was locked. I knocked, but my knock went unanswered so I sat down on the porch with my elbows on my knees, chin in my hands and waited. I really don't remember how long I was out there, but I do remember my feelings were hurt really bad. I wished I had gone with my cousins and sister then. I would like to say afterwards that she apologized, hugged and kissed me, but I don't remember any of that happening.

She used to tell me that I was a mistake. Not an unplanned pregnancy, but a mistake. It was her that told me I was a bastard. I remember thinking, "what is that". She explained it's a child born out of wedlock. Now what sane person tells their child that they're a bastard? Just to give another example, we took a family trip to Bush Gardens and she didn't seem to have time for me that day either. Not sure if it's the same day we lost my little sister or if that was a different trip, but this particular trip I wanted to spend time with her so bad I cried to get on a roller coaster with her. Of course I was too little and didn't measure up to the little man on the outside of the ride, but I cried so bad they let me get on the roller coaster with her. Keep in mind this was the 70's so they let me get on. When the roller coaster went into the loop I started to fall out. She caught me (I'm sure she regrets that now) and the operators stopped the roller coaster. To this day I don't ride roller coasters. I'm TERRIFIED of them!

As a little girl, turning into a young lady, my egg-donor never took the time to talk to me. I'm not sure if she talked to my sister or not, probably did since she was her favorite, but with me she just gave me books to read.

There was a series of books about a woman's body (development, menstruation, things like that) that she'd given me to read. Once I read it she asked if I understood, I said yes and that was it. Well, I started my cycle at 10 years old in the 5th grade. Of course I wasn't expecting it so I wasn't prepared and didn't have anything with me. I went to the school office and talked to the school secretary and asked her for a pad. Looking back on it now, it's really funny how it happened. I told her I needed to talk to her in private, then told her I needed a pad. She asked "a writing pad?" I told her no, a pad for your period. She said ok and got it for me, then asked if I wanted to call my mother. I said "no". She said "you don't want to tell her?" I told her, brace yourself, "No. The book said it was a private thing. I wouldn't have told you if I didn't need a pad." Well, 2 years later, 7th grade and 12 years old, I'm getting ready for school and my egg-donor tells me I'm not going to school that day, I was going to the doctor. I asked what was wrong with me and she said I should have started my period by now. I told her I'd started 2 years ago. When she asked why I didn't tell her I told her because the book about being a woman said it was a private thing. Then she asked how I get my pads. I told her I go in her bathroom and get them. I guess she was so into her husband and my little sister she hadn't noticed. She asked if I ever used a tampon and I told her no. She got a tampon and told me what to do. It went right up! And without any pain or discomfort. Now, in a normal person's mind, wouldn't that spark a question? Of course it would! Especially when your child is supposed to be a virgin! That was a clear indication that I was having sex. There should have been some difficulty or something if not. But wait, that means you have to actually be concerned about your child, right? Or, you already know in your heart what's happening and acknowledging what you just saw might make it real. She didn't stop and ask if I was having sex or anything like that. As a parent that would have been the next question, but of course she didn't ask. Needless to say, I went to school that day.

I've always loved to read. I started reading at a very early age and still have a love of reading. I don't know why we tell our children to "sound it out" when they're learning to read when we know the English language has words spelled in a way that you can't just "sound it out". If it's so easy why does the word phone have a "ph" instead of a "f". Of course I could go on all day with a list of words that are spelled nothing like they sound, but the word that affected me the most was "busy". My egg-donor beat my butt because of the word busy. I was reading, if I'm not mistaken, The Berenstein Bears, and the word busy came up. Well, I pronounced it "bus-ee". She kept telling me to re-read it and each time I said bus (as in a school bus) eee. She then told me to sound it out and of course I came up with the same thing. She whipped my butt! She told me it's pronounced busy (bi-zee). I told her if dizzy is d-i-z-z-y then why is busy not b-i-z-z-y. I got my butt torn up again. I wasn't being smart in the mouth, it just didn't make sense to me. She called my Daddy and he came over. I remember him bending down and taking me in his arms telling me it would be ok. That was long before she re-married so it had nothing to do with anyone else. It was just the way she was with me.

My sister was her baby and trust, me it showed. I've never been jealous of my sister, she was my heart, but I've always felt the difference made between us by her. I've always wanted children and used to tell God when I was a little girl that if He gave me more than one I would never treat them differently or like I was treated as a child.

I'm sure every child, well, most children are disciplined by their parents. That's a good thing. The Bible says that to "spare the rod is to spoil the child." Trust and believe I wasn't spoiled by her. Her idea of discipline when it came to me was to strip me naked, braid 3 switches together and beat me until I bled. Now it didn't take a lot to make me bleed, but I think she must have liked the sight of my blood. I would have "switch marks" on my body for days afterwards. Or she would strip me naked and beat me with a leather belt. Lots of times she would wait until I was outside with other kids, call me inside to beat me, then send me back out with the marks all over my body so it was obvious to others that I'd just got my butt torn up.

Still Standing

I felt like my sister was more like my child most of the time. Older siblings are supposed to look out for the younger ones, but I felt like I was responsible for her most of the time. With the shift my egg-donor worked I was home with her and when the nasty person she called a husband was home I wanted to make sure she was ok. Just in case he was looking at her the way he was looking at me. My egg-donor would leave a list of chores for me, especially when he and her would be out together. I'd wake up on a Saturday morning to a list and a note that they were gone for the day and to look after my little sister. Now again, it's only right that older siblings look out for their younger siblings, but let me share this.

One day, my little sister's bus came after mine so I stayed and made sure she got on the bus safely. I asked a neighbor down the street to take me to school and she said she would once she got dressed. While I waited I sat on my bed reading as I knew she would blow the horn for me. I closed the house up and was in my room when I heard the door open. Before I could get up to investigate I had a rifle in my face and my egg donor was screaming "where is he?" I didn't know who "he" was and I kept telling her that, but I was more concerned about getting shot in the face. I should have been used to it with all the guns the poor excuse of a man she called a husband had put in my face and mouth and other orifices, but I was still scared out of my mind. I managed to bolt past her and take off running out of the house and down the street. I was screaming "she's got a gun" and tears were streaming down my face. I felt like I was running at the speed of light. Flo-Jo didn't have anything on me that day.

I ended up at the house at the end of the road where an older couple lived. I finally got to the door and started beating on it. The old man answered and I told him she had a gun and was trying to kill me. Well, I guess she had enough common sense to put the gun down before she came after me and I guess my neighbor that was supposed to take me to school saw me running down the street because she never blew the horn. Either that or she saw a car come home. My egg-donor caught up to me, caught me in the collar and dragged me home kicking and screaming. I never understood why she would do that. Put a rifle in my face. But then again, the word "normal" doesn't apply to her. Even after all this time she still finds time to brag about putting a gun in my face. Recently, a younger cousin asked me if she ever put a rifle in my face because she told him she did and he didn't believe her. He asked me to see if she was telling the truth. Sadly enough she was.

Still Standing

Honestly, I don't remember what happened once we got back home. I thought she was dragging me home to shoot me. I'm sure there are a lot of days she wishes she had. Sadly enough, in my lowest hours, with all the hell I was going through, I'd started wishing she'd killed me that day, too.

After learning I was a mistake, a bastard and an ungrateful child because I loved my Daddy so much, I started to think death was better than living with her. And she prides herself in being a mother! Yeah right!

It wasn't until much later that I knew what real motherly love felt like. My grandmas loved me and I felt their love, but the relationship that a mother and daughter has is about as special as you can get. God knew I was in need of a mother, not just an egg donor. I longed for it and He gave me just that!

He gave me some real, undying, know when my child is sick, feel it when something is wrong, will hurt you if you mess with her, hanging out at the mall, laughing at anything, real love. I know I said real twice, but when you've been eating hamburger and finally get that ribeye, prime rib or filet mignon you truly know the difference.

I now have the mother's love I always dreamed of. It's even more wonderful than I imagined. My mama knows me, all my ways and will still get me straight and keep loving me. But she'll do it in such a motherly way that it's like a sigh of relief. It's a love that I cherish and I'm so thankful to God for.

It's one that I rebelled against at first because it was foreign to me, but thank God He opened my eyes to my answered prayer. I got, not just an awesome woman and mother, but an awesome woman of God. Sometimes we receive gifts and they're not gifts from God. We end up with any old thing and it may work, it may not. But when God gives you a gift, like when He gave me my mom, He truly gave me a gift and a gift that has HIS stamp of approval on it. A gift that had my name on it. What God has for me is for me! Everything happens for a reason. I'm thankful that God used my egg-donor to bring me into existence, but He was sending me and my mom the gift of each other when He did. He put His hand on it and it was done. When she walks into a room her presence is absorbed by everyone because of the anointing God has placed on her. When she talks, people listen. When she moves, people follow. It's because of Gods gifts.

He will truly give you what you need. He may not come when you want Him to, but He always comes on time. For what I lost, I've gained so much more.

When we were little, my egg-donor had a lot of animosity towards my Daddy. I think it was a lot of what I call "brokenness" that she hadn't dealt with when it came to him. She constantly told us how much he didn't love us, didn't want us and didn't do right by us. How he didn't take care of us and we were just conveniences for him. Now for a man who cared nothing for us, I remember he would come to my grandma's house and play with us, pick us up and spend time with us when she was at work. He also bought us things and always asked if we needed anything. I don't think she was supposed to know, but Grandma knew and did the right thing by allowing him to see us there. I remember Daddy giving me a birthday card and signed "love Daddy" but she'd gotten into my head so much I scratched the "love Daddy" out with a pin. Funny though, I kept that card for years. It gave me a sense of security, made me know that I did have a Daddy and that he did love me, even if it was being driven into my head that he didn't. I think, and of course I may be wrong, but I think she did that to make us her allies. Here she was, a divorced woman with 2 children (they were married for a brief time, though I'm not sure when they married or divorced), couldn't have the man she wanted and loved and one little girl that thought the sun rose and set in her and another little girl that, no matter how much she cried over her lost love, was still a Daddy's girl. I can't imagine that kind of resentment, but I'm sure she felt justified. I know what it is to love someone so much and they just don't love you like you love them. I know what it is to love someone and constantly get disappointed by him and never have what you wanted from him, but I don't understand how that animosity can be taken out on your child.

We all know that children aren't asked to be born into this world. We can't control who our parents are or to what environment we are born. I guess, with rose colored glasses on, I assumed that when a woman gets pregnant, whether planned or unplanned, that nurturing a baby is one of the most amazing experiences a woman can have. Now don't get me wrong, when a baby is conceived out of a stressful relationship, an act of rape or molestation or circumstances of the like, it would be hard. But for a man to, supposedly be your first love and your first, it just seems to me that the bond would be unbreakable. Regardless of whether that love worked out or not, the child is an innocent party. If you're not cut out to be a mother or just decide the time isn't right for you, please try the adoption route. There are women in the world who want nothing more than to have their own children and for whatever reason can't conceive or carry to term. Instead of abusing the child, give them up or give them to someone who wants to be a parent.

In my opinion, being a parent is one of the most precious titles we ever have. When we as children or even when our own children look back over their childhood, will they see it as something they cherished or something they want to forget forever?

There are pieces of my childhood that I cherish, but for the most part, I wish I could do it over. Well, I felt that way for the longest time. Of course, if given a choice, it would have been MUCH different, but I obviously didn't have a choice. None of us do. We play with the hand we're dealt. I'm at a point in my life that my glass, even the glass of childhood, I see as half full as opposed to half empty. I allow what I've been through, the way I've been treated and the lack of concern for me to determine what kind of mother I am to my own child. I want her to know that she means something to me and that she's my first priority. I want her to feel the way I never felt as a child. I want her to understand that being a mother means, first and foremost, loving unconditionally. That whatever attributes she does or does not have, is a perfect fit for her. And that I love her with all her perfections, with all her imperfections, with all that she does and does not do. I want to teach her by showing her that a Mother's love is the most precious love you can experience aside from Godly love. That she is a gift and her life is precious. I want her to know for herself so she can be an example for her own children, what a mother's love truly is.

A few years ago my family and I were traveling and after a while we stopped at a store. While my husband and daughter were in the store I had the pleasure of watching a mama and baby bird in the parking lot. The mama bird hopped along the parking lot looking for food with her baby on her heels. Each time the mama bird found a morsel of food, she would turn to the baby and feed the baby, then eat a bite herself. I watched this cycle, baby being nourished, then mom, for the better part of 10-15 minutes. I couldn't help but wonder this: This bird, this animal, had enough motherly love in her to take care of her child. She first made sure her child, a child she was blessed with and responsible for, was taken care of and it was her first priority. Genesis 1:26 tells us that God gave us "dominion over the fish of the sea and over the fowl of the air and over the cattle and over all the earth…." I had to wonder to myself, how is it that a bird will take care of their child but my egg-donor didn't see it as a priority to take care of me.

It was a hurtful revelation. I don't know why it hurt so bad on that particular day after experiencing so much hell, but then I realized a few things. 1-Reflection can sometimes be hurtful. 2-That time of my life was over. 3- God has blessed me with a beautiful child who will never have to worry about feeling that way. And 4- I WAS STILL STANDING!

Chapter 2: Going Thru Hell

Put your seatbelts on for "going thru hell". It's going to seem like something out of a movie, but then again, a lot of movies depict real life. Unfortunately this, in my case, is very real.

When I was very young, quite some time after my biological parents divorced and I was approximately 9 or 10, my egg-donor met what she considered to be a man. I guess in a few senses he was. He was of the male gender anyway. As a woman I know the difference between a "male" and a "man" and it's a big difference. My prayer for the women reading this is that if you don't know the difference, pray for discernment so that you will know. It will make a tremendous difference in your life. Back to the story.

They were introduced by my maternal grandfather as they were Masonic brothers. I don't know how long they were seeing each other but eventually we met him. He seemed like a really nice guy and even invited us all over for dinner one day and cooked fish.

Sometimes he would eat Sunday dinner with us at my grand-parent's house and it was what we thought, the beginning of something good. Other than that we had no intimate knowledge of him. There was never a time that we had outings for the 4 of us. They dated and we weren't included in their time together so we didn't have any intimate time to get to know him. Whatever time they spent together they were able to form a bond that didn't include us. We were one of those big family's that gathered after church at Grandma's house and had Sunday dinner. He would eat with us some times but of course there were lots of people around so he was on his best behavior as other eyes were there. Time went on and they decided to get married. I think I was in 4th grade when they got married. The wedding itself was nice and the reception was full of family and friends. Two things I really remember about the wedding was the cake (it was beautiful) and when I went looking for my egg donor, she'd left without saying goodbye.

She came by Grandma's later that night to say good-bye before they went on their honeymoon, but she'd left the reception without so much as a "see ya later" or anything.

I don't remember much after that about the reception because my feelings were hurt that she was gone and I didn't get to see her before she left the reception. I think I have an unconscious way of shutting down when I've been hurt. We moved into a mobile home in a small park after the honeymoon and everything was different. We didn't change our schools so my egg-donor picked us up from Grandma's every day when she got off work and took us home. We'd walk in the door all smiles, talking and saying hi to him and he'd be sitting there watching tv or eating. Once we walked through the door he would stop what he was doing, get up and walk into their bedroom without speaking. I thought we'd done something wrong, but it wasn't anything we were doing. He'd changed overnight. Literally.

From that time on whenever everyone was at home he was in their bedroom if we were in the main part of the house. If they were in the living room and we came out of our room to where they were he would walk out and go into their room. It seemed the strangest thing, but that's what we were dealing with.

I'm not sure how long we stayed in that mobile home, but from the mobile home we moved into a house in the country. When we moved into the house it was the same. He would have nothing to do with us or even talk to us.

One day we had a "family meeting" and she said she wanted us to be a family. I remember thinking to myself "why is she talking to us, he's the problem". Eventually he started warming up to us again, talking to us and watching tv in the same room with us. As time went on, he progressed to playing with us. That's when I started noticing "things". When he would play with us he would "tickle" me. Every child likes to be tickled, but his tickling progressed from under my arms and tummy to in between my legs and breast. Yes, I had already started getting them (breasts) and he was touching them under the guise of tickling. I was truly confused. I thought he was so into tickling me that he didn't realize his hands were where they didn't need to be. Then he wanted to tickle me all the time. I told him I didn't like to be tickled so he told my egg-donor I didn't want to play with him anymore. She then saw ME as a problem for not being receptive of him spending time with and playing with us. Even as a young child I knew that wasn't right, but she had a resolve to be with him and make him happy by any means necessary. Eventually I started back playing with him, but told him NO TICKLING. Even now I don't like to be tickled. One night we were in their bedroom watching tv. We were sitting on the floor and he was on the bed. My egg-donor was in the front part of the house. He eventually got on the floor with us and when my sister left the room (not sure if she went to another room or just to the bathroom) he deliberately rubbed my crotch. Then he stuck his hand in my pants and rubbed me where he had no business. I remember shaking like a leaf on a tree because I was so in shock.

No words came out of my mouth and no movement was made by me. I kept telling myself I was having a bad dream, but it was real. Very real and I was scared to death. He didn't say a word when he did it.

Eventually he started touching other places. He would catch me walking down the hall and make me stop so he could touch and rub me. I would stand there with my eyes closed, frozen in place, shaking in fear and ask myself "why is he doing this to me". Of course my actions changed when all of this started. I didn't want to do anything with him, I didn't want to eat at the table with him, watch tv in the same room or be anywhere around him.

Of course I was the problem now.

I wasn't being a team player and was fussed at because I wasn't acting like part of the family. Once again my egg donor sat us all down and we had the "being a family" talk again. I was the problem then and he made a comment to the effect of that's why he pulled away from us in the beginning because he knew that would happen. I realized at a very young age this man was very conniving. Of course he knew that would happen because he knew what kind of person he was and what he planned on doing. He told her he would make efforts to build a relationship with me. When she would go to the grocery store or leave the house going wherever, he would tell her to leave me there with him so we could bond. "Bonding" was touching and doing perverted things to me and he would always tell me that if I ever told anyone he would kill my little sister and my egg-donor. Eventually when she left the house I would beg her to take me too, not just my little sister.

She always said no. At that point I would go in my room and lock the door.

He always hit the door and told me to come outside. At that point I was subjected to all kinds of perverse things. When I would cry he would tell me I was making him upset and he would do bad things to me if I made him upset. I tried not to cry, but sometimes the tears just flowed.

Eventually, after I couldn't take it anymore, I told my egg-donor that he was touching me. She asked me what I meant and I told her. She said she'd take care of it and for the first time in a long time I felt like I had a mother. She went into her bedroom and closed the door. What seemed like hours later she came out of her room and told me we needed to talk. She said she asked him and he told her I was lying. That I just wanted to live with my Daddy and if I told her that then she would let me go. I started crying and told her I wasn't lying. She told me if I didn't get with the program and start being a part of their family I would be in trouble. She wouldn't let me play with my little sister for a long time after that and told me if I didn't eat at the table with him then I couldn't eat. If I couldn't be a part of them all the time then I couldn't do things with her and my sister. I stopped eating with them. I had no money and to this day I don't know the lady's name, but a lady at the school cafeteria fed me every day at lunch. She would also give me bags of chips that I'd put in my book bag and hide under my bed. I'd never told her what was going on, but God had given her to me as my "ram in the bush".

My guardian angel. When I didn't eat with them I would eat my chips in my room and keep the bag in my book bag to throw away the next day at school. I could get something to drink at home, but I had to drink it in the kitchen and not in my room. I hardly said anything to him or her. Only to my little sister when it was time to go to bed at night because that was the only time I was allowed to talk to her for a long time. I remember one night when she and my sister left and he wasn't there, she had fried some chicken and I was so hungry. I ate a piece of chicken, a chicken leg, and tried to hide the bone in the trash can. For some reason I thought she would see it so I took it out of the trash can, ran outside and threw the bone in the ditch. That would last me until I ate lunch at school the next day.

When I didn't get with the program and start "being part of the family" on the few times I wanted to be with my egg-donor and my sister doing things in the house, I wasn't allowed. I spent a lot of time reading in my room. I would get under my bed and read or get in the closet and read. Then, in my little child mind, I thought if I went to live with my Daddy everything would be perfect. I never in a million years thought she would say no. I thought I was a burden to her and she would be glad to get rid of me, but she said no.

She made sure to tell me that my Daddy didn't want to take care of me and that he didn't want me. Then she said I couldn't go. One evening she got ready to go and of course was taking my little sister with her. I begged and pleaded for her to take me with her. She told me no because I needed to talk to him. I told her I didn't want to talk to him, but she made me stay anyway.

That evening, I got another lesson in fear. When she left he told me we needed to talk. He had one of those old fashioned butcher knives with the wooden handle like my grandma had, and a gun. He told me that this was his house and what he says goes in his house. That everyone in his house would live by his rules and do what he says do. He also said that "what happens in this house stays in this house" and if I couldn't do what he says he could end it for me right then and be gone before she got back. He put the butcher knife to my throat and told me to choose. I could get my throat cut or get a bullet to the head, but if I was going to live, it would be in his house, by his rules. I was so stupid. I should have told him to end it for me, but for some stupid reason I wanted to live. I was a kid and I didn't understand that living in hell wasn't living at all. He told me when my egg-donor got back she was going to ask me if we talked and I was to tell her yes and that everything was fine between us. I'd never been more afraid

31

in my life! Mark my words, when people say "what happens in this house stays in this house!" it's usually some dysfunction going on. It's something they know isn't right, but don't want other people to know. Usually, not only do they know it's not right, but they condone the wrong being done and THAT'S the part they don't want others to know. It's a sad motto to live by.

When she got back home she asked me was everything ok and did we talk. I wanted to scream at the top of my lungs what had happened, but I knew I had no one in my corner. My answer was simply "yes ma'am". She was happy because she felt like her mirage of happiness was coming together and I on the other hand wanted to run away from there and go as far away as possible. That same evening I started making a sandwich and when I picked up the knife to cut the sandwich I started shaking. Until that day, the only experience I'd had with knives was for eating. I never in a million years thought one would be put to my throat. I made sure to compose myself quickly for fear he would be looking. I was 10 years old. After that life really went downhill. I was forced to "pretend" to be happy in a situation that was a living nightmare. I was forced to tell my egg-donor that I wanted to stay at home with him so it wouldn't look like it was his request only. The times she was gone and he and I were home alone together it was then that he was able to be himself. He was open to say the things he wanted to say, most of them perverted, and do the things he wanted to do with me and his actions were always perverted and included making me watch porn with him. It was obvious to others as well. A girl I went to school with had gone to a neighbor's house to visit and was going to come see me. The lady whose house she was at told her no, because he and I were there alone.

Even she could see it and she didn't live in our house. I thought about running away, but where would I go. My philosophy was "if your mother isn't there for you then surely no one else would be". I felt alone in the world and wondered why I was even born. I felt like I was the only person in the world going through what I was dealing with. I was made to walk down the hall at certain times so he could touch me. If I was late there was hell to pay. I was made to sit at the dinner and breakfast tables with everyone and pretend to be hungry and eat when really I was sick on the stomach from having to be so close to him. At times even now, I can still smell his cologne and it turns my stomach. One day, she left the house with my little sister and told me I wasn't going with her (again) and again I went into my room and closed the door. It had become a "no-no" to lock the door because if he couldn't just turn the knob and come in he would make the "shooting a gun" sign with his fingers. That was my sign that he was getting angry and I wasn't supposed to make him angry. Other times he would use a screw driver and take the knob off. This particular day he told me he had something for me. I truly didn't want anything he had, but of course I had no choice. He took me into the back bedroom after locking the screen and wood doors and the bedroom door and told me I was going to become a woman that day. I begged and pleaded for him not to do that to me, but he told me if I didn't go through with it not only was he going to kill me, but as soon as my egg-donor and little sister got back he would kill them, too. That their lives were in my hands. I cried terribly, but he kept saying women don't cry. I was far from being a woman. I was a little girl. There was a dresser, a piece of weight equipment and a bed in the room so I tried to focus on those things, but nothing would have ever prepared me for the pain and awful feeling that he was putting me through. If I had to describe it in one word, it would be HELL. I felt like my entire body was being ripped apart! I was 11 years old. I felt worthless, used and nasty and that was only the beginning. After that he made me stay home with him a lot more and every single time he would make me have sex with him. He always left me with "remember, don't tell or I will have to kill your mother and sister. You don't want that do you?" Honestly, I felt like she knew what was going on, but pretended she didn't. I felt like she was "giving me" to him to keep him there. I could be wrong, but there is no way in the world she could not have known. I don't understand why she never took me with her or why she never questioned why he always wanted me there with him. I realize sex is supposed to be fulfilling for both parties involved, but my first experiences were horrible. First of all, I was a child. There was no enjoyment, only pain.

He would want to kiss me like we were a couple enjoying each other. He would squeeze my face so hard and turn my face to his face to make me kiss him. He was so into what he was doing and I detached myself. In my heart and mind I always wanted to be a bird so I could fly away from there. I would concentrate on flying, actually flapping my wings and flying away.

Most times I would just lay there, but often times he would hit me and say "MOVE"! Sometimes he would wink at me like we had a special connection and it made me sick to my stomach. I know I often wear my feelings on my face so I'm sure the face I made in response to his winks told him I hated him. I assume he thought it was normal because he would ask me to say things to him. What the hell do you say? I'm a child! What am I supposed to say? Do you know this sick bastard would tell me what to say? When I didn't say it like he wanted me to, he would tighten his hands around my throat and make me say it like he wanted me to say it.

The abuse became a part of my life so much that I got to the point I expected it. I knew he was going to come into my room or make me go into their room when she wasn't at home. We had sex in their bed, in their bathroom, in my bed, the living room and the third bedroom. It was sick, but I was having sex with him almost every other day. It had become part of my "responsibilities". Wash dishes, do laundry, vacuum, keep my room and the bathrooms clean and have sex on a regular basis with this sorry excuse of a person that wants to be called a man. One night he had been in my room and when he heard her getting up he rushed out of my room. The instant he left I got a horrible leg cramp. I yelled out in pain and she rushed into my room.

Now, anyone with a nose should have been able to smell sex, but she just rubbed the cramp out. At the same time she rushed into my room so did he for fear I was telling on him. How I wish you could have seen the look on his face and could feel the fear that set in me. I thought he was honestly going to kill all of us in that instant. I didn't realize at the time that child molesters and men that beat women are actually punks. They put on a real tough act with a child or a woman, but put them against a real man and they don't stand a chance. I actually thought I would be his slave for the rest of my life. I mean, I had to keep everybody alive, right? I had to make sure my little sister was safe, right? I couldn't seem to get away from him no matter how hard I tried, cried or prayed. I felt like my life would be a grim existence and living no longer mattered. According to "the book", sex was supposed to be something 2 consenting adults enjoy together and it wasn't supposed to leave you feeling nasty, used and filthy. I wasn't an adult and it wasn't consensual.

At times his threat was that if I didn't "play nice" that he would do this to my sister. How could I let that happen? She was my baby. I had to sacrifice to keep her safe. There are several times I've wondered if I truly kept her safe. I never thought one person could shed so many tears. I felt like a filthy rag. I started my period when I was in 5th grade and at one point my cycle stayed on a lot. I was bleeding all the time and I was grateful because he wouldn't bother me if my cycle was on. My egg-donor took me to the doctor and asked about birth control pills to control my cycle. Now I'm sure as a woman you know things about a woman's body and being a woman and what makes our body tick, but I don't think I would ask a doctor about putting my 12-13 year old daughter on birth control pills solely for the purpose of her cycle. I could be wrong, but I felt it was his suggestion and like he said, what he says goes! I only took them for a little while and the abuse continued.

My abuser is such a conniving, sneaky person, the things he did to me I had no idea were in his sick, twisted mind, tests of loyalty. For example, I'm thinking I had to have been around 11 or 12, he called me out of my room one night and told me we needed to talk. He told me he was sorry for all the things he'd done to me and knew he couldn't keep doing it, but he couldn't bare the thought of me going on to be with someone else. He said he was going to kill me and kill himself. I remember having on a Strawberry Shortcake nightgown my Granny had given me. He took it off of me, stripped me naked, bound my hands and feet and taped my mouth and nose with duct tape. I hate gray duct tape to this day! I kept licking the inside of the tape to form a small pocket so I could breathe. This time as well, he had a knife and a gun. He put the barrel of the gun in my vagina, pointed it at my head and just kept pointing it at me in general. I think, in his sick mind, it gave him some kind of pleasure. He rubbed it over my nakedness and kept saying how sorry he was. I knew then he was "*apololying*", not apologizing.

After what seemed like an eternity of him touching me inappropriately, rubbing the barrel of his gun all over me and invading my body with his fingers, he untied me, took the tape off my mouth and put my Strawberry Shortcake nightgown back on. He told me he didn't deserve to live, but I did. He got on his knees, put the revolver in my hand and told me to kill him and then I could live my life without him bothering me. I HAVE NEVER IN MY LIFE WANTED TO PULL A TRIGGER SO BAD.

Now for all of you that doubt God, let me help you understand just how real HE is. While I was holding the gun, I heard a voice. Very quiet and very gentle and it simply said "put the gun down". I looked around and no one was in the room. I put my finger on the trigger and again the voice, very gently said, "put the gun down". I had no doubt it was God. I know how much I wanted to pull the trigger and splatter his brains all over the wall, but God said no. HIS voice isn't a big boom like they depict on the movies, but its gentle and quiet. I put the gun down on the floor, went into my room, closed the door and cried.

Many years later as I was going to trial, some of the other women that he'd abused in the exact same manner came to me.

One of them told me he'd done the same exact thing to her, but later told her it was a test of her loyalty to see if she would shoot him. That's what he was doing to me, too. Testing me. He let her know there were no bullets in the gun. Had she or me pulled the trigger he would have loaded the gun and killed us. I know how bad I wanted to pull the trigger, but God said no. What kind of sick person does something like that? The next day my egg-donor was fussing about the roll of duct tape in the living room. Of course he didn't own up to it, but I know I didn't take it there. Of course I was blamed for it and had to put it up. I shook so bad having to touch it and again, to this day, I HATE GRAY DUCT TAPE.

Of course the abuse continued and I tried my best to be a normal teen-ager, but as I got older I realized I had no clue of what normal was. My childhood was anything and everything but. I'd been a great student before my life changed with all the abuse, but I still ended up being a decent student. Just decent. Oh I was smart, but other things were on my mind aside from school. Wondering if I was ever going to be free of the situation, wondering if my egg-donors eyes would ever be open to this situation or wondering if she would ever acknowledge what she saw right under her nose. Loving someone is one thing, but being completely stupid is something entirely different.

Let me give you an example of the stupidity I was dealing with. I'm sure if not you yourself, you know someone whose job or company has had an "open house". You know, the day that your family can visit your job for a family fun day, cookout and see the workings of what your loved one does at work. They're on a Saturday afternoon and some companies even bring in bounce rides for the children or different activities for the family. Well, he told her his job was having their open house in the MIDDLE OF THE WEEK and he was entering me into the spelling bee for the event, BUT, she couldn't come. Really? What company has open house in the middle of the week? She checked me out of school and drove me to the city he worked in to meet him as he didn't work in the city we lived in. Is it just me or does it seem that she was "giving" me to him. It only takes a little bit of common sense to survive. Now, what person in their right mind wouldn't question that? An open-house at your job, in the middle of the week and the only person allowed to come is the little girl that he keeps wanting to be alone with. Hmmm. Ponder that for a minute. If that doesn't have stupid written all over it, just stop reading right now.

Of course we didn't go anywhere near his job, we went to an abortion clinic. You see in all of the abuse he managed to get me pregnant when I was in the 8th grade. I was a skinny girl and it was obvious that I was pregnant, if you cared to look. My egg-donor walked in the bathroom on me one day and noticed my enlarged mid-section and asked if my period had come on. When I told her no, her response was simply when it came on I had a lot to get rid of.

I guess he figured if he told her he was taking me to an open house for a spelling bee that would be enough to slip past the stupidity. I guess he was right. He might as well have said "I've been molesting your daughter, got her pregnant and I need to get her to an abortion clinic before she gets too far along". We went to the clinic and he filled out all the paperwork and paid for it. He told me he used his mother's address on the paperwork because he knew no one there would open his mail. He didn't pay for anesthesia though because I felt everything. It felt like someone reached in me and just yanked my insides out and vacuumed out all they couldn't grab with their hand. Before he made the decision to take me to have an abortion, he gave me names. If it was a girl her name was to be Charlene because the mother of the daughter he could acknowledge wouldn't name his daughter that and if it was a boy his name would be Cedric. Because I was so young and in such an abnormal situation, I thought if I actually had a baby the baby would be the only person in the world to love me. I didn't feel loved by anyone else in my life at the time and surely a baby, my own baby, would love me unconditionally. I'm thankful everyday that I don't have a child by him. In my youth and excitement over having someone to love me, I wrote the names on two balloons. I got in trouble with my egg-donor for writing a boys name on a balloon. Nothing was ever said about the little girl's name on the other balloon.

We went to the clinic and after the procedure was done I was in a lot of pain, but he refused to have the prescription filled because it would draw attention to what had been done. Later that night my Grandma picked us up to go to church with her and I cried all night long at church. She thought I was "happy" or filled with the spirit. Little did she know I was filled with pain and an ever-growing desire to take my own life. Here I was sitting in church, but going through hell. Later when we went to court we touched the subject of the abortion, but didn't proceed. The nurse from the abortion clinic showed up at the courthouse to testify as a witness on my behalf after reading about the trial in the newspaper. I had a chance to talk with her and she told me she knew in her gut that something was wrong that day. She suspected what happened all along and came to be supportive and even testify if necessary. Ironically, the abortion wasn't allowed in the trial. They decided because of my age it would be inappropriate. They also decided the defense may try to hire boys or men to come and *testilie* that it could have been their baby and thus cause reasonable doubt. With or without allowing it in the trial, there was no doubt I had been raped and abused by my so called mother's husband and the charges were real. Because the information was inadmissible in court, I debated over whether or not to put it in the book, but I stepped out on faith and decided to do it. Not to overwhelm you, but to help you understand a spoonful of the things I've had to go through in this situation. It was obvious to others that I was pregnant, but the person that I lived in the house with never acknowledged it.

When my great-grandfather died (egg-donor grandfather) all of us were sad. I was even more sad because my life was in shambles and I wanted to be the one in the casket. I couldn't figure out how to get out of the abusive situation on top of dealing with death, which I don't do well at all. I was thinking about having to go back home and deal with all the hell I was going through. The thoughts overwhelmed me so much so that I fainted at the funeral. I'm sure my family may have thought I got too hot, but the thoughts going through my head were really overwhelming.

When I came to I was in the back of the church with my aunt and she was standing over me. She's a Jehovah's Witness so she wouldn't sit with the rest of the family, but stayed in the back of the church. I felt strange, but I thought to myself at least he won't come into my room tonight knowing I've fainted today. Well, I was wrong.

I began to wonder and ask God why me. I wanted to die all the time, but never at his hands. Suicide was an ever-present thought and I'd be lying if I said I didn't try it a few times in my life. If a boy in the neighborhood paid any attention to me, he would always come in my room with a gun and threaten me. I've had more guns in my face and mouth than any one person should ever experience, but this was his way of controlling me. Fear and control.

Abusers get off on controlling their victims and trust me, he had control over me. When the opportunity wouldn't come for him to actually come in my room with the gun when he was mad at that moment, he would sit at the kitchen table and clean the gun. That was my "warning" that he was upset.

He would tell me things like I was nothing, wasn't ever going to be anything or have anything. Candi Staton has a song, "God Can Make Something Out of Nothing" and that became my theme song. Some of the words are; "if all of your life somebody told you. You'd never amount to nothing. Then somewhere down the line, you began to believe. So you started to act, just like nothing. You took the easy way, but look where you are today. God can make something wonderful out of you." I love that song.

I used to sing that song all the time. Sometimes aloud and sometimes in my head and heart, but that song got me through. Somehow, somewhere in the recesses of my mind, when I wasn't thinking about suicide, I knew I'd make it.

I wish I could say at this point that the abuse had stopped, but it hadn't. I'd been being abused since I was 10, lost my virginity at 11, had an abortion at 13 and was trying to figure out what normal was and why I was being given to him because it felt like I was being handed to him on a plate. By this time my whole sense of who I was wasn't anything a teenager should be thinking. I knew I wanted to be loved, but also felt I was "tainted" and not worthy. The summer before I went to high school I was at my Daddy's house one weekend. We would go over there sometimes and there was a longing in me that didn't want to leave, but I always went back home for fear that my egg-donor and sister's lives would be in jeopardy. I'd gotten a little bold with my abuser, especially when I was in the "I really don't care if I live or die" moods I would often be in. I would make smart comments because I knew whether he was angry or not he was coming in my room. Whether he was angry or not he might bring a gun and he might not so I didn't feel I had anything to lose. I told him the next time I went to my Daddy's house I wasn't coming back. Well, I was sitting on my Daddy's front porch and felt something whiz by my nose. In the same instant I felt something whiz by my nose I heard tires squeal and then a shatter. Instinctively, when I felt the "whiz" I leaned back and in the next instant my Daddy's car window was shattered as it was in the driveway right beside the porch. The glass had been shot out. That was my "warning" and I didn't even talk to my Daddy about living with him permanently or tell him I knew what happened with the window or who had done it. If I had sneezed or sat up less than an inch I wouldn't be here writing this today. Needless to say I went back home. I know its wrong, but my Daddy found out what happened to his car when he read the manuscript for Still Standing.

At times we would stay with my Aunt and Uncle in the evenings while my egg-donor and her husband worked. I loved being there because it meant I wasn't home. Anywhere but home was where I wanted to be. My little cousin didn't like going to bed at night so I would lay down with him so he could fall asleep. When my abuser got there at night to pick us up I would pretend to be asleep. In my little child mind I thought that if I was asleep he would leave us there or at the very least send my egg-donor to pick us up. Anything to not have to go home with him, but of course it never worked. He would whisper in my ear "I guess it's her turn tonight" and I would jump up from a fake sleep so he wouldn't hurt my sister. I never wanted to kill him more than when he made threats about my sister.

Years later that same Aunt and Uncle called me to their house to ask me didn't I think my abuser had been in prison long enough. That I needed to do what was right and have him released. My Uncle and I had gone outside to the car to talk about it. I told him exactly what I thought and why he was exactly where he should be. I realize there are people that are unjustly incarcerated, but he should have been there a long time ago and as far as I was concerned my egg-donor needed to be there as well for neglect! If that wasn't a classic case of neglect I don't know what was. My Aunt informed me that our family had been torn apart and it was all my fault. She said God would reveal the truth and I would have to go to my family and apologize to our whole family for being the one to tear it apart with my lies. I was the victim, I was the child. No one ever thought this could be true? Do you really know this person as well as you think you do? He had the whole family fooled. Well, most of them anyway.

By this time, I'm in high school, things at home are hellacious and I'm so ready to either leave or die I just don't know what to do. I'm wondering if I'll ever be free from this life of abuse or be a normal person. I'm in 9th grade and this is supposed to be a great time of life for a young person, but I was miserable. I want, with everything in me, to reach out to my egg-donor and it's just not working. She's doting over my little sister and it's obvious in her actions that she's only doing what she has to with me. She is so in love with this man she can't see straight, even though he would leave for a few days and not call or tell her where he was. I remember her sitting and watching the phone waiting for it to ring and we all know a watched phone never rings. All she wanted was him and to make sure that all his needs were met. I understand wanting to make your husband happy, but when it comes down to a choice of a man or my child, my child wins every time. A grown man can take care of himself. Children do not ask to be here.

Again, my mouth gets me in trouble. I try to go to HER and ask for her permission only to live with my Daddy. She went on and on about how he didn't want me and how I wouldn't be happy living there, but when I told her I'd rather take the chance and find out for myself, she somewhat conceded. She told me I could go at the end of the school year. I wanted to go right then, but she said I had to wait. I think me wanting to live with my Daddy and not her really hurt her. I really don't think she was concerned about my feelings at all. I think she felt like yet again, I had chosen my Daddy over her and I think she worried about how it would make her look.

When she finally told me I could go she seemed defeated. She would come home and talk to my sister, but wouldn't talk to me. I knew she was hurt and I wasn't trying to hurt her, I was just trying to get out of a horrid situation. When my abuser realized she'd conceded to letting me go live with Daddy, I'm sure his twisted mind started ticking. I'm sure in his mind he thought if I really went to live with my Daddy I would tell everything he'd done to me. Honestly, I had no intention of telling. I just wanted to get away from him and their house.

One night, very shortly after her agreeing to let me go stay with my Daddy (mind you I hadn't mentioned it to my Daddy yet because of what she'd been saying to me pretty much my whole life) he started calling home constantly. If I would answer, he'd hang up on me or breathe heavily in the phone. If my sister would answer, he would ask to speak to me then once I came to the phone do the same stupid thing. I WAS TERRIFIED! I called my Daddy that night and told him I really needed to talk to him. He could tell I was upset and wanted to come get me right then. I told him if he did it would get really ugly, but to please meet me at school the next day. I thought if he came to their house she would have him arrested and then he wouldn't be there to help me. He made sure to re-assure me I would be ok and he would see me the next day. Now, if only I could make it until the next day.

In my teenaged mind I thought my abuser would kill me and when my Daddy got to school the next day and found I wasn't there he would start looking and asking questions and find out I was dead.

I was truly not prepared for what would happen that night when he got home. That night, he reminded me of our original conversation where he told me this was his house, I was going to be there and if I didn't want to be there it would be either by bullet or knife to the throat and I'd chosen to stay.

Now I'm trying to leave and it wasn't going to happen. After slapping me around a lot he put a knife to my throat and started making cuts. He wasn't cutting deeply at that time, but he was choking me and cutting. Hitting me and telling me how I was a liar because I told him I would never leave. He told me I wouldn't see the next day. That he was going to kill me and leave. He had a bag packed and had rented an apartment in

Wilson, NC. He would be there a short time before he left to go to Kentucky. Of course he didn't have to worry about me telling anyone because I would be non-existent by the time he made his escape. By this time he was really choking and cutting me BUT, let me tell you about God. My egg-donor used to get off at 12 midnight but, around 10 pm that night lights turned into our driveway. It was her! For whatever reason she'd gotten off early and was at home. He slapped me, told me to go run water over my face and get back in bed, but to know that it wasn't over. I did it so quickly I was back in bed by the time she put her key in the door. Psalm 46:1 "God is our refuge and strength, a very present help in trouble." That was God!

When she came in she stuck her head in the bedroom door and called my sister's name, but didn't call my name. Yes, my sister and I, most of the time, slept in the same room. She used to sleep so hard she would roll into her covers and fall on the floor and never wake up. Her covers were a cocoon around her and she was a very sound sleeper, but I have to admit there were many times I wondered if she really and truly slept through all that was going on.

Still Standing

She (my egg-donor) was hurt because I wanted to live with my Daddy and really didn't want to talk to me anyway. I knew then that if I didn't get out of there I wouldn't be alive much longer. The next day I rode the bus to school and one of the guys kept asking me what was wrong. I told him I couldn't tell him, but all I needed him to know was that if something happened to me "he" did it. He kept asking questions, but of course I didn't tell him what happened. There was also a girl that rode my bus that was somehow connected to my abuser. She was all in my conversation with the guy and kept saying over the seat "I already know what happened". For some reason, if a boy liked me in school, he knew it. If a boy talked to me in school, he knew it. Somehow, they were connected but I've never known how. She and I were the same age, but she felt it ok that her mother and her double-dated with men her mother's age. I guess normal is what we get used to. I assume they knew him and had some type of relationship with him.

Again, that's just my assumption. I see her now and all I can do is pray for her though she thought my predicament that morning was quite funny. Her lifestyle shows all over her.

Now how is it that he, the guy on the bus, could look at me and see bruises and that something was wrong, but my egg-donor was up when we left for school and didn't notice. It wasn't that she didn't notice, she just didn't care.

At lunch, I went to the commons area of my high school and waited for my Daddy to show up. When I saw him I asked him to walk outside with me.

We walked in front of the school to the flag pole and he asked me what happened to me. I unbuttoned my shirt and opened it so he could see my neck and chest area and all the cuts and bruises. He grabbed me and asked me who did that to me and when I told him he took me by the hand to his car and we left school. I told him if he got home and my sister was there and I wasn't he would kill her so we picked her up from school so he wouldn't get home and realize something was amiss. Even though I was going through I was still in "big sister protection mode" and needed to make sure she was ok. At that point I knew I was safe and that horrible man wouldn't bother me anymore.

Chapter 3: And a Little Child Shall Lead Them

Thank you Jesus, at this point I know in my heart the abuse is over. I'm with my Daddy, he knows that something is wrong, he just doesn't know to what extent. At this point we're on the way to the magistrate's office. We saw my grandma in traffic on the way and Daddy stopped her and told her to get her daughter and meet us at the magistrate's office downtown. My Daddy went in and talked to the magistrate until my egg-donor got there. Once she got there, Daddy confronted her about me and all hell breaks loose. They're going at it like it's another world war. I remember her telling my Daddy to give her her child and she would take me home and handle it. Fear set in instantly because I thought I would have to go back, but my Daddy told her I was never going back there. It got so ugly the magistrate kicked us out. I felt so guilty! I felt like I had hurt her and was going to cause her and my little sister to lose their lives. I cried all night and waited for the call that they were dead. Well, I'm sure if she had gone home and responded like a real mother I'm sure they would have been. But when you go home and tell the poor excuse of a man you call a husband that all is well and you're on his side then you are no longer a threat.

Ok, from here on you get to hear my Mom's involvement in all of this. You will see the difference between a real Mother and an egg-donor. To give you a little insight, my Mom, not my egg-donor, and Dad got married when I was in the 8th grade. Honestly, I'd known her since I was a little girl, but she and Daddy had been together for a long time before they married. The bond between us was formed long before the "I do's" were said.

We go home and the next few days are spent "detoxing". We have doctor appointments, decisions to make and I have to try to sleep. My parents are doting over me to make sure I'm ok and I'm trying to adjust. My mom is taking off work, taking me to appointments, going with me to different appointments and holding my hand for support through it all. Ironically some of my medical records had "disappeared" by the time we went to trial, but we still had enough evidence and documentation to proceed.

Daddy was super supportive, too, but I think he was trying to stay out of jail. What real father wouldn't want to put a bullet in this poor excuse for a human?

Still Standing

At this time in my life sleep is absent and it's still a very rough time. My mind is in so much turmoil and I'm so scared I can't sleep. I'm wondering when he's going to show up, when I'm going to catch a stray bullet, when I'm going to get the call about my egg-donor and sister being found dead and I'm honestly wondering how long it will be before he makes good on his promise to kill me. I had to change schools, also. Keep in mind I didn't "check out" of school that day, I just left. By this time rumors are flying. It's being said that I'm changing schools because some of the other kids at school didn't like me or because some them wanted to fight me and even that I got into trouble at school so I had to move. It was even said I used a nail file to cut my own throat. Really? If someone had come to me with something so trivial I would have laughed. Hmmm, let's see. Some kids at school don't like me OR getting constantly raped, threatened and mistreated at home. I don't think I would have cared about some high-school girls not liking me with all I had going on. And I wasn't a trouble-maker and didn't stay in trouble so it just told me that people needed something to talk about.

At this point I'm getting comfortable in my new home. I feel somewhat safe, but still worried he will see me somewhere and shoot at me. One of my aunts, egg-donor's sisters, called and asked to speak to me. When I got on the phone she cursed me out for taking her sister through this. She really let me have it and I started crying uncontrollably. She made sure to tell me how wrong I was for lying and taking her sister through all of this. Again, the child, the victim, was unimportant. What I had gone through was irrelevant. My Daddy took the phone and hung it up, but again I felt like a filthy rag. The way I saw it, others were hurting and it was all because of me. I was really wishing I was dead now. Me, the child, was supposedly the root of so much pain for so many other people.

I started at my new school with a lot of my old friends. You see, when my egg-donor first got married we stayed at the same schools. When we moved to the house in the country we changed schools. I finished my 6th grade year in the same school and changed in the 7th grade. When I changed schools I became "the new girl". Now I was back in school with the kids I'd started out with. Most of the kids were the same, but a few new faces had been added. I felt like they could look at me and see that I was "different" or weird in some way. Except one person. She befriended me and we're still best friends. By this time we're freshmen and it's been a while since I've seen them. I'm trying to be normal, but also realize I don't have a sense of what "normal" is. I felt like I was walking around with this huge dirty secret.

Well, truth be told, I was. At this point I still haven't told my parents about the sexual abuse. They're still trying to get me adjusted and coping with the information they know.

My mom is clinging to me closer than ever. We used to go to Gramps house on Sunday evenings and for the longest time, I sat on the floor at her feet. She was always rubbing my head or touching my back with that re-assuring touch to let me know she was there. It felt so good, but it was foreign at the same time because I'd never received that kind of attention. We went everywhere together and did everything together and I knew that was what I had been missing all my life. She doted over me like I was a baby. Actually, I was her baby and I didn't feel anything but love. I now had 2 loving parents that not only told me they loved me, but showed me. It was something new and I loved it. I've always loved pizza and for the longest time I thought it was her favorite, too because we ate it regularly. What I later found out is that she likes pizza, but we ate it so much because I loved it. It may have been small to her, but to me it was a great showcase of her love for me.

One night my Daddy and I were watching tv together and I asked him a question. The question basically was this: If you know someone is in trouble and you know something else about them that will get them into more trouble, do you tell on them. My Daddy looked me in my eyes and told me to always do the right thing. When we do the right thing good will come out of it. Always do good and always do the right thing. At that point I teared up and told him everything. That was the 2nd time I saw my Daddy cry. The first time was when his Grandma died and even being a young child I knew how much he loved her. Now he was crying again. He didn't cry in front of me, he went into his room, but when I walked by his door I saw him crying. I told him about the touching, the threatening, losing my virginity at 11, all the different guns I'd seen and been threatened with, the forced sex and beatings. As a parent now, I know that's more than any parent, well any real parent, can handle knowing their child had to endure. As a parent now, I'm sure my Daddy wanted to kill him. My mom was at a meeting when I told him so Daddy had to tell her later that night. How do you open your mouth to say such a thing? How do you form the words? How do you as a Mother receive that about your child? It had to be just as devastating for them as it was for me.

But like he told me, he did the right thing. We pressed charges and my world became filled with a DA and assistant DA and statements and legal assistants and victims assistants and a bunch of legal things that were making my head spin. It was truly another rough patch in my life, having to go over what I'd endured over and over. I couldn't sleep and felt like everyone could look at me and see what I was going through. I went to a doctor who tried to teach me "mental sleeping techniques". Sometimes they worked, sometimes they didn't. Here I am a freshman in high school, hoping and praying for some normalcy and it seems to be getting worse. Believe it or not, my abusers daughter, niece and nephew went to school there as well. We always spoke and smiled in passing as at that point no one knew what was going on. Then, they arrested my abuser. From my understanding it was all on the news. The arresting officers said he had a "superman complex" and considered it a difficult arrest. But, he was in jail and for a minute I felt a sigh of relief. The next day I was talking to my step-sister at school when her cousins and a bunch of other girls came and pulled her away from me. They told her that her father had been arrested and it was because of me. Honestly, I think she's hated me ever since. I mean, that's her dad and if she's anything like me she loves her dad and sees him as a super-hero. Maybe, just maybe, if the shoe was on the other foot I'd have feelings of hate, too.

For one year I went through legal procedures, counseling that I really and truly wasn't receiving at the time, statements, investigations and a lot of other things no child should have to go through. Of course he and my egg-donor maintained his innocence the entire time. Even now, they're both still telling that lie. Officers went to their house and seized all the guns in the house, even though he and my egg-donor said there were only 2. An old rifle his deceased father had given him and a hand-gun. Officers were amazed at all the guns they removed from that house. They were right where I said they would be and I'd endured a horrid experience with each and every one of them. I had to ask myself if my egg-donor really thought there were only 2 guns and was in shock when they found all those guns or if she really knew they were there. I truly don't think she knew about them. Why would one household, unless they're avid collectors, have that many guns? Then, did she ask herself why there were that many guns in the house?

This was becoming very real and it was difficult to get through. One day my Mom and I were at home and the phone rang. She'd become very protective of me and would answer the phone first. She told me one of my cousins on my egg-donor's side of the family wanted to talk to me and everyone knew how close we are. With all the negative calls I'd been getting she wanted to make sure I only received calls from people who were supportive. I went to the phone thinking I would get a chance to talk to my cousin, but I wasn't prepared for the voice on the other end. It was him- my abuser! He told me to call this off, tell everyone I was lying and he'd never bother me again. I started screaming "it's him, it's him" and my Mom came and took the phone from me. Of course when she got on the phone he hung up. She pulled me to her and held me while I cried. She comforted me and held me until I was ok. Now that's a real Mother. When Daddy got home she told him what happened and he too, made sure I was ok. He, my abuser, had made bail and I guess at this point the situation had become real to him, too. He'd gotten away with abusing me and so many other women that I'm sure he felt invincible. That is until the tables turned. He was no longer in control. He could no longer use fear and weapons to control me. Don't get me wrong, I was still in a very terrified state of life, but he didn't know it. Here I was a child, to our knowledge, the youngest person he was abusing or had abused and I was the one to say no more to the point of pressing charges. I'm sure he had to think that with all the women he'd abused when they were children and got away with, that he could go on doing it forever.

There is nothing special about me, nothing at all, but God used me, a little child, to stop this abuser from continuing to do the filth he'd been doing for years. And He moved mightily with some of the other women so that they came forth too and said "yes, he abused me too".

One year later we had our first trial. Yes, first of three. It would be a long time before this nightmare would be over. In the year it took for us to go to trial several women came forth that had been abused by him. All of us told the same scenario. I guess abusers sometimes do things in patterns. Just like most people put on both socks then their shoes, this abuser had the same MO with the women he abused. Of all the women that came forth only one of them testified, the woman that conceived and birthed a child as a result of the abuse she'd endured at his hands. Sadly, that's how her child found out who her sperm donor was. And as beautiful as she is she looks just like him. More so than the children that he can publicly claim. Can you imagine being put in the position of having this wonderful, amazing little person, but at the same time have mixed emotions because of the way the child was conceived. That HAS TO BE a bitter and quite large pill to swallow. Though he denies ever touching her, DNA has confirmed that he has. Where is her justice? Where is her back child support?

Psalm 59:1 "DELIVER me from mine enemies, O my God: defend me from them that rise up against me.

At this point, we're in court and going through this hellacious trial. My egg-donor is making "I hate you" faces at me across the courtroom while he's making "I'm gonna kill you" faces at me. I'm in 10th grade and spending quite a bit of time out of school to be in court. Somehow, I managed to make it to the 11th grade. When you go through something like this you truly find out who is for you and who is against you.

Again, my aunt, one of my egg-donor's sisters, told me that our family had been destroyed and it was all because of me. She would pray that God revealed the truth and then I would have to apologize to the family for tearing it up. I had cousins I'd grown up very closely with, stop talking to me and even lie on me. One of them said I told her I'd read the story in a Readers Digest. What she didn't know was that my Daddy was a subscriber and had every copy of RD from the past 10 years. Of course, every edition was read with a fine tooth comb and guess what? Nothing like that was anywhere to be found.

The family that had been so close forever was now torn apart because members were choosing sides and thus a huge division formed. Again, I felt guilty.

Not only did I have to testify about all the sick, sordid, unnatural and nasty things I'd been through, but so did the other woman who came forward. In the end we got a conviction and he was sentenced.

Psalm 140:1 DELIVER me, O Lord, from the evil man, preserve me from the violent man.

My prayers had been answered. We got a conviction and a sentencing and for a minute I could breathe a sigh of relief. My life would start to find a place of normalcy. Or so I thought. I found out my Pastor, my self-appointed god-mother, and my Mom & Dad were my biggest allies. Them, along with the other VICTOR that had come forth. I think her coming forth helped her start a healing process and I was truly grateful to meet her and have her in my corner.

I mentioned my "self-appointed" God-mother. She's a woman that I saw every day and from our first meeting made an impact on me. She actually cares about me and I wasn't getting a lot of that at that time. She had no idea what was going on, though when I told her about the birth control pills I'm sure she began to wonder about it. She's an awesome woman that by caring for me, had her life interrupted with subpoenas and court time. Can you imagine the sheriff constantly knocking on your door, missing time from work and having to be a witness for a trial that has affected so many? Yet she still loves me and is still my god-mother, loving me unconditionally. Thank you Mama B!

I wish I could tell you that was the end, that I found a sense of normalcy and started the healing process, but that would have been too much like right. My abuser and egg-donor were able to get an appeal on the grounds that there is a seven year statute of limitations on rape and molestation. Thus, the argument was that the testimony of the other woman helped him gain sentencing and was thus inadmissible. In other words, he was a free man.

I had to then prepare myself to go through the entire trial process again. Can you imagine finally getting the courage to stand up to your abuser, tell your child she was conceived from an act of rape and allow her to know all that happened to you, only to find out the law deems it "unimportant" because he got away with it for over seven years? Where's the justice in that? If a person is murdered and the murderer gets away with it for 20 years, they can still be charged 20 years later. The victim is no longer here to deal with the stress of what happened but with the arrest the victim's family feels a sense of justice. If a person is raped and the rapist gets away with it for at least 7 years the judicial system deems it "unimportant". Charges can't be pressed after 7 years. Where's the justice in that? I think the judicial system needs to re-think that statute of limitations.

It's my Junior year of high school and here we go again. We're back in court and I'm missing time from school again. Of course, the missed time is excused, but I'm missing valuable class time and I'm having to keep up on my own.

The stress is more than a teenager should have to endure. It's bad enough to have gone through the ordeal, prepare for trial, go to trial and then have to go again. I thought the process would never end. Well, we go to trial for the second time and guess what happens? We got a hung jury. 11 to 1. We went through an entire trial, re-living the nightmare all over again and this is the result? Can you imagine how hard of a blow that was? It was later said that the "hung juror" said she had to live through her abusive ordeal so I should have to live through mine. Can you believe that? Here I am, 16 years old, a junior in high school, had been going thru hell since I was 10 and now this! I wanted to die all over again.

I think this decision helped to strengthen my abusers "superman complex". Who do I say that? Well my Mom and I were in the mall one day and I'd finally gotten the nerve to venture from her shadow. I went to the other end of the mall and he was in the mall.

When I saw him a look of fear came over me and a look of "I told you I'm gonna get you" came over his face. I started running and he started running after me. Adrenaline had me running at warp speed and he didn't catch me. I ran to my Mom who was at the opposite end of where I started running from. When I got to her I was screaming that he was after me and when he saw that I had run to her, he stopped chasing me and walked by us laughing. By this time my Mom had pushed me behind her and stepped up like she was ready for battle. Can you see the difference between a real Mom and an egg-donor? The difference is a clear as day!

I had to decide if I wanted to go through with yet another trial. I was certain at that point I had to. I couldn't stop fighting. If we didn't end up with a solid conviction it wouldn't be because I gave up. The thought came to me that if this man wasn't convicted, not only would he eventually kill me, but he would continue to abuse women. Who knows, he might even get crazier and kill his victims instead of having them take him through that process again. I told my parents I wanted to go through with yet a third trial. By the time we got to trial for the 3rd time I was a senior. I had suicidal thoughts, I wanted to kill my abuser and my egg-donor, but somehow I still felt somewhat sorry for her. For some reason, in my heart, I'd taken on the role of the adult. By that I mean I was more concerned about her feelings than she ever was for mine.

At the same time I truly hated her. I hated her for not loving me, I hated her for being there for him and not me and I hated her for what I felt was deliberate disregard for me. And I hated her for being weak Again, I'm missing days and instruction time from school, my head is spinning with all that I'm going through, I've gotten lazy in my schoolwork when I am in class and I don't want to do anything.

But here I am in court again. I'm having nightmares in the few hours I am sleeping and I'm feeling like if this doesn't work out this time I have a date with a large bottle of pills.

At one point I took a gun with plans of ending my life. I didn't want to live anymore and I felt the world would be better off without me, but I couldn't go through with it and told my Mom what I had done. She told me I had to keep fighting. And I did just that!

Throughout the whole ordeal the media is having a field day with the trial and I'm now being ridiculed by some of the kids at school. I'm wondering will I ever get to a point of "normal". But like old folks say, "God may not come when you want him, but HE'S always on time". We got a conviction!

Thank you Jesus! No loopholes, no statute of limitations and no more trials. It was finally over. Two life sentences plus a few more years for all the years of hell. It was all worth it. The bad part was with all the being unfocused, going through trials and wanting to give up, I didn't make my grade. One class, missing 2 points in that class and a teacher that could care less had me not graduating. I own my part in it too. I would have to graduate in summer school. I was so hurt and out-done. I didn't get to graduate with my class, but again, I didn't give up.

I took the course in summer school and graduated with the handful of seniors from all the local high schools that for some reason or another, didn't graduate with the rest of their class. It's over. No more trial, I have a diploma and I start trying to focus on having a normal life. And even though I often doubted I would make it, I was STILL STANDING!

Chapter 4: It Is What It Is

At this point in my life, there's no court, no high-school and no drama from the abuse. I've had a few relationships, but now I've met the man that I would soon marry. He knows I come from a lot of dysfunction and he decided he was here for the long haul. I'd been having a lot of mixed emotions about my egg-donor and was trying to figure out how to have a relationship with her. My mom was awesome, but for some reason the little girl in me still wanted my egg-donor to love me. By this time her so-called husband was in prison and I was thinking she actually might be able to think for herself, but I thought wrong. Quite a few times her response to my efforts was "my husband said you're not welcome here" or "it's not a good idea for you to come here anymore" or "it's not a good idea for us to talk. My husband wouldn't approve." I reached out to her a few times and it was touch and go. Sometimes we were able to get along, but for the most part we didn't. I found myself trying to spend time with my little sister at her house and sometimes she'd be there.

When my boyfriend asked me to marry him and I became his fiancée, I decided I wanted her to be a part of it. I went to her house and told her I was getting married. I didn't want or need her money, but when I walked down the aisle I would like her to be there. Of course my mom would be on the front row after having lit the unity candle, but it would be nice if she was there. She told me that as far as she was concerned she only had one daughter and wanted nothing to do with me. She also told me that I was getting a husband and that was something she no longer had because of me. Can you say hurt? And that's my fault because nothing she'd ever done when it came to me had any other results. But I was truly hurt. I left her house blinded by tears. I got engaged in June and by December I was married. Instead of a wedding we eloped and the next day I went back to work. An associate of hers saw me and noticed I had 2 rings on. She asked me was I married (dumb question) and when I said yes she asked me was my egg-donor there. I'm sure the look on my face told her all she needed to know so like a little kid she ran back and told her I was married. Who do you think showed up on my doorstep that weekend with tears in her eyes?

You guessed it. My egg-donor! She was upset that I had gotten married and she wasn't there. Now I began to understand; this woman had to be bi-polar. But stupid me, I felt sorry for her. Before we eloped I'd bought a wedding gown so I let her go with me to take pictures in it. There wasn't a need for it anymore, but I wanted some pictures. She went with me and the photographer took some nice pictures. Shortly after that she asked me could I please tell people that I lied so her husband could come home. I was crushed. Believe it or not, I kept trying with her and at times she would initiate it, but it always boiled down to "please tell them you lied so my husband can come home." It was never about me. It was always about him. He always came first, he was her priority and he was who she missed in her life. Not me. It was never me. After a LOT of trying and getting the exact same responses, I put on my big girl panties and left her alone. For a long time it wasn't enough that my Mom and Dad loved me or that my friends loved me or that my husband loved me, I still wanted to be loved and accepted by her. I later realized it was about loving myself. Even though there was something deep inside me that felt I deserved to be loved, a tiny part of me felt like I was truly a mistake. I mean she'd told me that since I was a very young child. Maybe, just maybe, if I hadn't been born she would have been happy. She would have had my little sister years later and life would have been great for her. She would have had that daughter whose every thought of her would be positive, whose eyes lit up when she thought of her and who, regardless of what she did, would be in her corner. Maybe, just maybe, I wouldn't have had to go through what I went thru and all would be well. But Jeremiah 29:11 reminded me, " For I know the thoughts that I think toward you, saith the Lord, thoughts of peace, and not of evil, to give you an expected end." To me, that means I should expect great things, being loved and to prosper.

With or without her I am what God says I am. And it is so awesome without her. Without her there is no constant reminder of the hell. Without her there is no roller coaster ride of emotions. Without her there is no disappointment.

Without her there is no deceitful intent. Without her there is peace and I cherish peace. That little girl desire is gone. All that I didn't get from her I get tenfold from my Mom and its awesome. For what I lost I gained so much more. I learned that all parents aren't real parents. I learned that your surroundings don't have to make you who you are. It's your determination that makes a person who they are. That your environment should not be used as an excuse to fail, but a platform to stand on while you succeed. I've also learned that success comes in personal measurements.

Someone else's idea of success may not be the same as mine. The fact that I have a sound mind and can function as a normal person is success I'm thankful for each day. When I take care of my family instead of following the initial example that was set for me that's success I'm thankful for each day. Demanding respect and carrying myself so that others will want to respect me is a success I'm also thankful for on a daily basis. In the words of the great Aretha Franklin, "R-E-S-P-E-C-T, find out what it means to me". Exactly! Find out what it means to me and every person you deal with on a personal level. Please know that respect is judged on a personal basis. What I consider respect someone else may not. One big thing respect means to me is not judging at all. You can never tell what a person has been through and I'm so thankful that I don't look like what I've been through.

I'm thankful to God for sending my Mom to me and giving me ALL that I lacked and then some. I'm thankful for someone that said, "this is what a young lady does and this is how its done the right way" and not only telling me, but living it so I can see the example. I no longer miss what I thought was good for me. I'm also thankful for a real dad. Not every man would have done what my Daddy did. Not only did he take me away from her, but he's been one hell of a dad. A real man. And as far as my egg-donor is concerned, truth be told, I have no emotional ties to her at all. That may sound harsh, but it's true. In my world, she no longer exists. It goes back to the old adage, "fool me once, shame on you. Fool me twice, shame on me." Well, shame, shame, shame, shame, shame……………… on me! But not anymore! You can't make people be who they are not and more importantly who they don't want to be. Psalm 24:10 tells us that "when my mother and father forsake me, the Lord will lift me up." HE is truly who we have to depend on and trust me I've learned to trust and depend on HIM. And in the words of Maya Angelou "when someone shows you who they are, believe them." It's just that simple. The bottom line is we have to know who we are and who we are in Christ. I know I'm not perfect. I'm a long way from it, but I like me. And if no one else in the world does, it's ok, because I do. The bottom line is, IT IS WHAT IT IS. And guess what, I'm STILL STANDING!

Chapter 5: Brokenness

A ccording to the dictionary, broken is defined as "reduced to fragments; ruptured, torn, fractured; not working properly". Usually we think of things or objects as being broken, but people can be broken, too. I, myself, to a certain extent, am broken. Brokenness can come from different things. Failed relationships, lack of communication in relationships, non-connected parent/child relationships, low self-esteem to name a few. We know low self-esteem can come from a multitude of things that happen in our daily lives. Losing a loved one or a job or having issues on your job as well as your home life can also cause brokenness.

I could go on and on, but in my case, my brokenness came from a sordid childhood, no real relationship with my egg-donor, being made to feel like I'm worthless or a mistake and being told I would never be anyone or anything. In society's eyes or statistically speaking I should be a basket case.

Walking the streets in search of a false sense of reality (drugs), selling my body, in a nut house, unable to function or having another woman as my significant other, but God said otherwise.

Let's start at what I know to be the root of my brokenness, my egg-donor. Can you imagine being pregnant at 16 by supposedly the only person you've ever loved, having visions of spending the rest of your life with this man and end up being a single parent? I'm sure a lot of you reading this can imagine it because you've been through it. It's not easy. Your heart is broken in a million pieces, you have this baby to be a mother to and now you feel like you're alone. I ASSUME that's where her brokenness began. Trying everything in her might to keep this man and get him to love her back. When after she's done all she knows to do, she still doesn't get the prize.

We've all been there. Lost love is a very painful experience, but it's HOW we handle that hurt/brokenness that's important. When we don't deal with our brokenness, it turns into a sore. Each time we're hurt that sore gets bigger and bigger. We begin to ask ourselves, "what's wrong with me?" We look in the mirror and start listing all of our faults and those faults, in our minds, are the reasons we're not loved the way we desire or feel we should be. Then we settle for anything. I know I'm guilty. Anywhere we can feel love we walk through those doors and often times it's the wrong door. It only leads to more hurt. Her brokenness, accepting what she felt like she could get (this is just my opinion now), is what lead to my own brokenness. The "mistake" she felt she made in loving this man, I feel like, caused her heart to feel that the "mistake" of a baby was a result. People say everyone is entitled to one "mistake", right? But then that "mistake" seems to favor the one thing that you feel has hurt you the most and that just pulls the scab off and pours acid on it. Thus, I was labeled a mistake and reminded of it quite often. That's a great example of brokenness. In my eyes, her "settling" for a piece of man in a no-count person took me through the door of hell and thus my brokenness issues. I've looked for love in the wrong places, wanting and needing to feel love. My sense of love was skewed, but of course I didn't know it at the time. My heart and mind told me all the things that were wrong with me. All the reasons why no one wanted to truly love me. Or told me they loved me then left me. It had to be something about me that made others not want to love me. I was "tainted". That brokenness led me to end up in places, with people, in situations and beds I should have never been in. Sex is not a substitute for love. I learned that lesson the hard way. Young ladies, soon to be wives and mothers, wearing sexy or provocative clothes is not the way to get attention. Of course if your clothes are hugging your body, not just form fitting, but actually hugging your body, and your cleavage is saying "hi" to everyone you encounter and your skirt is so short a gust of wind will put all your goodness on display, you are sure to get attention. But is that the kind of attention you want? Males and females alike will pay attention to you but with what intent? Maybe, just maybe, if your hair, in whatever style you choose, is neat and clean and your clothes fit, not hanging off of you, but fit and are appropriate you will still get attention.

Your nails are done, not in need of repair or the polish is chipped. Simply filed neatly or shaped is good. If your feet are out and the crust is gone and the nails are either polished or at least neatly filed that suggests that you've taken time for yourself. You will still get attention, but instead of the wrong attention, you're getting the right attention. People will actually look at you and think, "now there's a rare find, a lady". Not a woman, not a girl, but a lady. Trust me there is a difference. When you carry yourself as a lady, preferably a woman after God's heart, that is what you will attract. A man, preferably a man of God. Think about it.

And for the young men, soon to be husbands and dads, carry yourselves as young men. Wearing your pants below your behind is not swag. It's a "prison mentality" that says you're "willing to be taken from the back". That you're "available". Yes, all the hip rap stars are doing it, wearing their belts to hold their pants up on their legs instead of their hips, but why? Quite a few of them have been to prison, maybe that's where they really got the notion from. Ok, that was a funny, but really. How would you run if your pants are wrapped around your legs? I'd like to see that. It would be my laugh for the day. Honestly, picture it. It truly is funny. Wear your clothes in a way that a true lady or a true young lady would think to herself, "now that's what kind of man I want on my arm". If you don't have any children why would you call everybody "son"? If you do have children and the person you are addressing is not your child, please don't refer to them as "son" unless you are speaking with someone you consider a son. It doesn't make you look cool and it doesn't make you a man. Talk to people, especially ladies, the way you would want someone to talk to your mother.

When you carry yourself as a man, especially a man of God, that is what you will attract. A woman, preferably a woman of God. When you carry yourself as less than a man, that is what you will attract, less than a woman. Think about it. I don't know who that was for but it poured out. I wish someone had told me those things at a very young age.

It's a long road to "undo" all the brokenness that's been done in my psyche. Even now, there are days that I look in the mirror and wonder how to undo the brokenness. At times, my husband can tell me how beautiful I am to him and how much he adores me and I still wonder why he feels that way. It's not every day that I think that, but there are some days I do. Or all I CAN see are my short-comings and it eats at me. I have to remind myself that I deserve his love and to be happy. I have to remind myself sometimes that I'm not ugly. Some days I have to remind myself that I should have great things in life and that God doesn't make junk. Then I can go on a little farther. Sometimes I wonder if my egg-donor can see her own brokenness. Is her blatant neglect of reality her coping method? I wonder if she really acknowledged what has happened will she be able to handle it. I mean, I'm a married woman and sleep beside a man every night. I may not know the exact minute he gets up, but eventually I know when he's not in bed. There is nothing in me that makes me feel like, not only did she know he wasn't in bed, but what he was doing when he was not in bed. Your man is constantly not in bed and you never get up? Is that because something in you knows what's going on, but if put right in your face you can't handle it? Again, this is just my thought. When you are already broken, i.e. reduced to fragments, i.e. torn, i.e. not functioning properly you may feel that just one more thing will completely crush you to the point of non-existence. That maybe, just maybe, her telling people what she cooked him for dinner last night, what they watched on tv and things they are presently doing is her way of coping. Her way of NOT breaking beyond repair. Living in the fantasy of him being there with her when she and everyone else knows he's in prison, creating what she considers a real relationship in her mind is probably her way of coping. I don't judge. I don't understand, but I'm not judging.

This brokenness I feel comes at different times and places in my life. Like years ago when one of his sisters ran me off the road. Or when another of them keyed my car. On top of that, I get confronted in the parking lots of public places because of all the brokenness he has created. Well, I am no longer that scared little girl anymore and I will not lay down and be defeated in any way, shape, form or fashion by anyone. I'm more than that.

Once I was at a dear friend's house to help her celebrate her birthday. She's an older lady, old enough to be my mother and I think the world of her. There were several people there and one lady kept staring at me. When I left, she told my dear friend that I shouldn't be in her house because I'd told a huge lie and said that my Daddy raped me. That she knew my Daddy and knew it wasn't true. Ironically, this friend of mine knew the whole story without me telling her. Long before we knew each other or I knew who she was, she'd been a court house employee during the time of my trials.

Ironically, she knew who my family was, including my Daddy and knew her friend didn't have the story straight or know what she was talking about. She was simply spreading gossip and told her so. Please understand that people who gossip come in all ages and don't have anything better to do with their time.

When she told me about it I was crushed. It helped me solidify the fact that a lot of people will have a lot to say about the situation and about me. Most of them truly don't have a clue what they're talking about, but it used to break me all over again. But you know what I realized? These people have not walked one mile in my shoes. These same people doing all this lip service may not have been able to walk in my shoes or even slip their feet in them. The Bible teaches us we shouldn't go to our brother about the speck in their eye when we have a plank in our own. Until we deal with our own planks we don't have room or time to worry about anyone else's speck.

(Luke 6: 41-42). That brokenness that we carry and spread to others will soon cause more brokenness. The cycle has to stop. At some point we have to act accordingly. Not be perfect of course, but think about what we say to or about others. Do you know what it feels like to have almost your entire family turn against you? Now I'm not saying that each of my family members spoke out against me, but for the ones that did, realizing I was not who they chose is hurtful. Let me explain. Throughout all the years this went on many, many family functions had been planned. Family cookouts, anniversary parties for my grandparents, birthday parties for different family members…all of that and more went on with me not included. When it came time for a family event to be planned it always came down to the decision of which one of us to invite, me or her. Who do you think they chose? Yep, you guessed it- her.

Later, as some of my familial relationships started to mend, I was shown pictures of my family at different events and realized I wasn't invited or wanted at those events. I was the child! I was the victim! Why was I punished? It was very hurtful. I missed so much and so many positive family gatherings because I was the problem, I was the outcast, I caused the division so I had to be the one to exile. I was the "black sheep" of the family. Not only does it affect me, but it affects my husband and daughter. Everything is supposed to be ok and we are to open our arms and say "come on, treat me like I don't matter and I'll keep smiling in your faces and keep holding my hurt in". My child may not know the hurt, but my husband sure does. It was him that took me to my egg-donors house once he proposed. It was him that was there, waiting outside when I ran out of the house in tears. It was him that kept me from running blind into a car because I was so hurt by the words my-egg donor had just said about me not being her child and not wanting anything to do with me. That I was getting something she no longer had because of me. It was also him that answered the door when she showed up with tears in her eyes because she wasn't there when we got married. Brokenness affects not just one person, but it's like a cancer that spreads through the family. The damage isn't just "skin deep". It affects all members of the body, the body being the family. When we were in attendance at family functions it was always the "can't you just take a picture with her for us" or "can you two please try to talk" or "can she take a picture with your baby- she is her grandmother". No she is not. All of that is stupidity to me. . Forgiveness and stupidity are two different things. If you flat out refused to take care of your own child what makes you think I want you anywhere near mine.

I'm nowhere close to being perfect nor is anyone I know. I've turned the other cheek again and again and again and again and yes, it still hurts at times. Only one that walked among us was perfect and HE now sits at the right hand of the Father. HE is also a healer. I am asking HIM to help me overcome my brokenness. There are times I KNOW He's doing it because I know it's not me. On those days I don't hate my hair or the reflection in the mirror. It is at those times when it is truly one set of footprints in the sand. And when I've built enough strength to stand on my own two feet, I know in my right and wrong He's beside me and the only reason I am STILL STANDING!

Chapter 6: Forgiveness

orgiveness. WOW. What a simple word with such a huge meaning! Often times, when someone has wronged us, we find it hard to forgive. Even when we say we forgive, we often make reference to the wrong that was done to us. That's not true forgiveness. I'm not saying you truly forget, but you discount that which was done to you. A long time ago I thought I had forgiven my egg-donor, but soon realized I really hadn't. If I saw her in passing I could barely stand the sight of her. She physically made my stomach turn and that's too much power for one person to have. Of course she didn't know she made my stomach turn, but not only did I know it, I felt the bile rise up in my mouth. I'd kick myself constantly for allowing her, even though unbeknownst to her, to have enough power to make me physically sick. I know I have every right to hate her, and I don't mean just a strong dislike, but strong hate. I hated her for birthing me, I hated her for never making me feel loved or in the few times she did the bad strongly outweighed it. I hated her for loving a male more than me, her own flesh. I hated her for taking his side and fighting for and with him tooth and nail and I hated her for being so weak. I could go on and on with a list of reasons why I hated her, but its way too heavy. Hate is heavy. It is a burden heavier than either Sampson or Paul Bunyon can carry, yet I carried it. And for years I carried it not realizing it was such a heavy burden. Truth be told, I loved hating them. I never broadcast my feelings, but if asked I parted my lips and with a strong voice said I hated them and meant every word of it. Do you know how hard it is to live a lie every single day of your life? I was like that comedy/tragedy mask. I was miserable at home, but when I stepped outside of our four walls the mask came on. I smiled and went about my business like I was just as normal as the next person. Really, my heart was broken and my mental state was a melting pot of emotions, but I went on, doing what I had to do. Surviving. Hate had become so much a part of who I was and my whole being that it was just who I was. Now don't get me wrong, I'm not a mean person or a person with a nasty attitude. Most of the time I look at life with the glass half full as opposed to half empty. I've even tried to maintain relationships with loved ones knowing my love for them far outweighs theirs for me. Knowing my intentions towards them were good and them not caring one bit about me or my feelings. I no longer do that. I love my family, but let me help you… just because someone is your mother, father, grandparent, sister, brother, aunt, uncle, cousin.....does NOT mean that person has your best interest at heart. Believe that!

Quite a few people, I won't say most, are out for their own personal gain, regardless of the title on the relationship. Self-preservation far outweighs loyalty. I have learned that lesson well.

Last year in June, I was put in a position to be in a room with 2 ladies. These women are not only awesome women, but they're awesome women of God. They both, for one reason or another, knew my story. These women talked to me about forgiveness. I won't say they preached to me, but they talked to me in depth about forgiveness and not only how it will benefit me as a person, but how it was God's will for me to forgive. That forgiveness was not for them, but it was for me. Now don't get me wrong, I have some awesome examples of God's love in my life. My Daddy, Mom and different people I've known throughout my life are awesome gifts of God, but for some reason, at this time, I think God was saying "enough" and used these 2 women to infiltrate my spirit. I was with them on a Tuesday afternoon and when I left their presence I was at war with myself. My spirit and flesh were clashing so much my skin broke out in a rash. All over my face, lips and arms broke out. I was so ugly! Stress, confusion and turmoil took over my body. I couldn't sleep and when I did I dreamt.

Tuesday night I dreamed about her, my birth mother, my egg-donor. We were sitting at the very unique kitchen table my Daddy had when I was a little girl. I remember the table because I used to love the pattern in it. She was sitting at the table with a very calm demeanor and I was in the kitchen.

She looked at me and said "I know, but I can't admit it or it would make me look bad. Besides, I love him." In the dream I jumped across the table to attack her, but of course that's when I woke up. Needless to say I didn't sleep much that night. The next day was rough and I wouldn't even talk to God. I was in so much turmoil I wasn't sure if HE would hear me. That night (Wednesday) I dreamed I was walking along a trail with Jesus. We were just walking and talking and it was AWESOME and so peaceful. At one point during our walking conversation HE turned to me and said "if I wanted to take you with me right now, and all you had to do was say the words "I forgive him" would you do it?" I started screaming "Yes, I forgive him!" over and over. Then I woke up. Woke up with my heart and mind in turmoil. Flesh battling my spirit. I tried to open my mouth and say the words, but my flesh was winning big time. By Thursday I was exhausted!

My spirit and flesh were still at war and the battle was being elongated by my stubbornness. Did I say I was exhausted? My church had Bible study on Thursday night, but my flesh was willing me to go to bed and pray for sleep.

At this point I'd started taking pills to sleep and it still wasn't working. I pressed my way to Bible study and it was good. Just as Pastor was ending he said "hold on, turn to James 3". I feel like that was Gods' way of telling me to stop saying I hate him. To watch my words and be careful what I say, so I stopped saying it. I still felt it, but no longer said it. Trust me I'd said it enough in the previous week to wallpaper a shopping mall.

Friday night I went to bed with an internal battle raging inside me and I felt wiped out. If you've ever been a cartoon watcher the words were circling around my head like a cartoon. I could read the words internally, but found my flesh literally pursing my lips together to keep them from coming out. I dreamed about it all night, the words circling in my head, the battle of good verses evil, right verses wrong wearing me out as if was indeed engaged in a physical battle.

Saturday morning I woke up gagging and vomiting clear liquid. Not sure if I was choking on the words or the devil was trying to take me under, but I began to ask God to help me say the words. I felt weighed down all of Saturday and ended up laying down around 4 p.m. Sunday morning was 5th Sunday and we didn't have service on 5th Sunday. I awoke much earlier than normal and started flipping channels. I found Joel Osteen (I love his ministry by the way.) on an odd channel. It wasn't TBN or any of the other channels he usually comes on, but he was on this channel. Far be it from me to remember what the channel was, but I remember thinking it odd for him to be on that particular channel. He spoke of Jacob's daughter, Dinah, being defiled by She-Chem. He went on to say how Jacob's sons slew all the men in the land as a result. At that point I felt his, Joel Osteen's face, fill the screen and he looked right into my eyes. He said "even when you've been defiled, you have to move on, do what God has intended for you and receive your blessings. That God has blessings for me but they won't be released to me until I move on." Can you say goose bumps? I got a chill, but that flesh….OOOHHHH! My lips still wouldn't say the words. That little cartoon sign was still scrolling through my head, but my head and lips weren't on one accord. I prayed, asked God to help me get there and went about my day.

Monday evening I was bent over in the sink shampooing my hair, the cartoon sign still scrolling around my head. I was hoping the sign would get wet and go away. If only it could, right? Of course, I couldn't be so lucky.

(By the way that was a joke) Then again we don't operate on luck do we? Blessings are the streets we take and leave the avenues of luck to other folk.

All of a sudden, the words "I forgive him" slipped out of my mouth. At first I paused and thought, "did I just say that?" But when my mouth opened again, it came out again. Now for some stupid reason I thought when the words finally came out of my mouth I would pass out, vomit, fall… something. Isn't that stupid? But nothing happened. I pondered on it while I did my hair (oh the hair was a mess because I was too consumed with the words of my mouth instead of the hair on my head-but it was clean) and realized I'd truly said it. I texted my husband and told him the words had come out of my mouth. I let him know I was crying, but I felt they were happy tears. Then the tears dried up and refused to come anymore. Later that night while I was in the mirror attempting to salvage my hair I actually smiled at myself. I'd really said it. I'd accomplished something as hard as pushing a boulder uphill, in the rain, wearing 4 inch heels. When my daughter and I said her "night prayers" as we do every night (we say The Lord's Prayer) as I recited it with her, it took on a new meaning. I've been praying that prayer for years, but that night God opened my eyes to it. I wasn't just reciting anymore. I felt full, like crying, but not sure why. I could feel the tears building up, but they wouldn't come. They even welled up in my eyes, but wouldn't roll.

Now because you forgive someone, especially knowing that person means you no good, doesn't mean you have to deal with that person or be a part of that person's life. It simply means you've forgiven them. A few days later I was having a conversation with another awesome woman of God and she likened me to clay. When a potter is working his clay, he adds water. Well, the tears rolled then. God allowed me to cry at the drop of a hat. He was beginning to re-work me. I didn't wear mascara for a few weeks. My spirit was in a mess of transition and there was no need to look like a raccoon because my spirit was in a mess. I know my Mom would say, "waterproof baby girl, waterproof." Also, a tired came over me. Not my normal tired, but a tired like my body needed a deep sleep. I guess I was mentally, spiritually and physically fatigued. I'd been in a spiritual fight and it had wiped me out. I felt when I came out of that deep sleep my sight would be different. Not my physical sight, though a new pair of glasses wouldn't hurt, but my spiritual sight. The next night I said it again, just to make sure I'd really said it before. Kind of funny that I had to check that, huh? I forgave him and her and I even prayed for them. I can't say that I've fully forgiven them, but I can say that I'm on the right road now. Understand that forgiveness is for me, not them. I thought it had come quickly from the time I'd started going through the battle, but in reality it has taken over 30 years. I was 10 years old when the touching started and now I'm in my 40's. That's a long time to carry hate. I'm making steps instead of standing in place. But in order to make steps you have to be in a standing position. Thanks be to God I'm "STILL STANDING"!

Afterthought

WHEW! This has been a journey. Re-living all of this to write this has truly been rough. Once I read through it and realized all I DID NOT put on paper, all that happened that isn't being published, I'm truly thankful that I'm here. In the words of Miss Celie from The Color Purple, "I may be black, I may even be ugly, but I'm still here!" There's no way I can tell every little detail. Yes, it's just that much! Not only has this affected me, but it has affected my husband, our child and our family life. It determines places I allow and don't allow my child to go or things I don't and do allow her to do. It has affected my parental actions and my actions as a wife to my husband. There are things I did before I met my husband that had I not gone through this abuse I'm sure I wouldn't have done. Things I thought were normal or acceptable that I would never want my daughter to do. Things I've been a part of that I thought were ok that I would never ever want my daughter to be a part of. With renewed vision I know they're not things I'm proud of. I know through grace, pain and suffering that I want my daughter to have so much more than that.

I didn't want to put so much negative in this that you don't receive the blessing from it. So much that you get stuck in the muck and the mire and never get to the healing. I don't want you to think this is about, as I fore-mentioned, putting someone's business out there. As you see, there are no names in this book. The intent is not to slander anyone's name or to create a negative atmosphere. The whole intent is healing. COMPLETE HEALING. Trust me, this has been harder on me than you, the reader, will ever know.

I started back having night-mares while getting through this and found my "mommy protection powers" went into overdrive, but it's ok. I'm still standing. Why did I do this you say? What purpose did it serve? Why would I go through all of this again? Again, the answer is healing. My healing and to help others heal. And when God wouldn't let me sleep, nudging me to write, I figured I'd better be obedient. Trust me, this is nothing I wanted to do.

Often times we go through something and feel we're the only person in the world it's happening to. Truth be told, we're not alone. Someone, somewhere can relate to whatever it is we're going through, even when we don't think so. The subject may be the same, but it happens differently every day with each person that's affected. Prayerfully, this book will help others at least start the healing process. It has helped me. I've cried and I've smiled knowing this was a "cleansing process". I've smiled in revelations that I don't think the same way I once did. I've smiled in the mirror at times because I know I'm a different person and even with all my faults I am still a child of God. My prayer is Still Standing will give others the courage to fight. Fight their abusers and not allow anyone to have control over them.

Fight the demons we have from being victims of abuse. Fight for what we know is right and deserve and that's JUSTICE. I'm truly convinced that the devil tries to "snuff out" the gifts God has given us. When we roll over and allow that to happen we have been defeated, but when we FIGHT, we not only take back what is ours we put the devil under our feet. When we put the devil under our feet, we have victory over the enemy. You wouldn't believe what my fight entails. Until recently, I went before the parole board every year and with a strong voice told them why the person that abused me should remain incarcerated. Until recently, he came up for parole every year after being sentenced to multiple life sentences plus more years. I don't agree with that because to me life should be just that. LIFE.

Now the governor of this great state says we only have to do it every 2 years. Many letters and petition signing went into that decision and I still have more letters to write. Can you imagine what that's like? I'm supposed to be at a point in my life that all of that is behind me and it's not. When the date comes up I have to mentally prepare for it, re-living the ordeal through sleepless nights and nightmares. It takes me to a low each and every time, but I'm working on that. I pray then go before the parole board and await a response. It's not a good feeling. All that fighting and I'm still having to fight, how unfair is that? Going through all that hell, fighting in court for three years and finally getting a solid conviction, shouldn't that be enough? I should be able to close that chapter of my life and move on, but I can't. I refuse to give up. He's not had any infractions in prison, but then again, there aren't any little girls in prison. I refuse to give up and will do everything in my power to keep that particular rapist in prison. If slaves had given up the fight for freedom, blacks would still be living in bondage. If women had given up fighting for equal rights we would still be "barefoot and pregnant" and where would society be without us? I can't give up either. If I give up now, to me that's like saying I don't trust God and I do. He created me to be a fighter. That thought takes me to the excerpt from Marianne Williamson's Book "A Return to Love, Reflections on the Principals of a Course In Miracles."

"Our greatest fear is not that we are inadequate. Our deepest fear is that we are powerful beyond measure. It is our LIGHT, not our DARKNESS that most frightens us. We ask ourselves 'who am I to be brilliant, gorgeous, handsome, talented and fabulous?'. Actually who are you not to be? You are a child of God. Your playing small does not serve the world. There is nothing enlightened about shrinking so that other people won't feel insecure around you. We are all meant to shine, as children do. We were born to make manifest the glory of God that is within us. It is not just in some of us, it is in everyone. And as we let our own light shine, we unconsciously give other people permission to do the same. As we are liberated from our fear, our presence automatically liberates others."

How powerful is that? So no, I can't, I won't give up.

It was prophesied to me several times that I would write this. Even the Lord Himself let me know it was a book in me. I boldly told him NO. Want to make God laugh? Tell Him what your plans are. Jeremiah 29:11 "for I know the plans I have for you…". Well, as you can see, HIS plan prevailed.

There is still a lot of brokenness inside me. I have to work on mending myself or at least be open to God mending me. I am more open now and realize I am a work in progress. Not a pot ready for use yet, but I'm getting there. God is slowly, but surely taking me out of my comfort zone. I'm not sure I'm ready for it, but I'm willing. Even though I've forgiven, animosity still lives inside me. Prayerfully that spirit will be evicted from me. It gets hard sometimes knowing the one person I thought as a very young child would always be in my corner is my prime enemy. Hiring private investigators to prove I'm lying only to find more women that have been abused by him. Her very own investigators finding yes, more women the poor excuse of a man she calls a husband has abused. Yet she doesn't believe them either. Contacting The Innocence Commission and having them try to get him vindicated. Working diligently to get a child molester and rapist released from prison so he can continue the trend. This same person who stands faithfully and proudly by a convicted rapist, loudly claiming his innocence and supporting him every step while lying to co-workers about what they watched on television last night or what she cooked him for dinner. She knows just as the people she's lying to, that he's in prison and I pray that it's for exactly what the sentence is- LIFE. So yes, it gets hard dealing with the animosity sometimes, but I have to remind myself that God is in control. He sits high and looks low and has all of this in His hands. He reminds me as I've said before, that forgiveness is for me, not for them so I have to keep walking in it.

You wouldn't believe the number of people that ask me "is he out?" When my response to them is why are they asking me that, they proceed to tell that she told them she had to get home to cook dinner for her husband or how he was standing in the door when she drove up to their house or what they did together the previous weekend. I simply tell them no he's not out and pray that the stupidity and dysfunction isn't hereditary.

I had the opportunity to read their appeal for the case. Not the first one, but the second one. Keep in mind we went to court three different times and the first appeal was granted for there being over seven years since he had raped and molested the other woman that came forth. The second appeal stated that he didn't touch me before I was thirteen and that would change the sentencing. Not once does it say he didn't touch me, just that he didn't do it before I was thirteen. Now, with your wife proudly by your side you appeal on that ground and she still remains supportive of this BLEEP BLEEP BLEEP. You fill in the blanks with your own words because I got real creative right then. Forgive me for being human and letting my emotions get the best of me, but how utterly trifling is that? We already know how trifling he is because he likes to sleep with, threaten and abuse little girls, but when you choose to support him knowing that he has abused your child, how trifling does that make her? Yet, I pray on a regular basis to continue to walk in forgiveness.

I thought about being raised in the church having to hide so much. Church is where we go to cleanse, release and seek healing, but I never did that. When I was going through it I kept it all inside. I probably could have received an EMMY for making everyone around me think my life was normal when really I was going through hell. After the initial release and being rejected and told I was lying, I kept it inside and it was a cancer eating at me. I prayed, often times asking God to take me, but HE had other plans.

Rape, molestation and abuse (mental, physical and sexual) are all tricks of the enemy. I've been through it all and I'm still standing! It's not me. It is only with the help of the Lord. I can't begin to tell you how many times I've contemplated suicide. Do you know how often I've tried? There are a lot of hurtful things in this world and the things I've been through are no less hurtful than what someone else has gone through. Healing is in order for all of us.

Betrayal is something I've experienced since I was 10 years old. I EXPECT it because I know its coming and it has yet to disappoint me. Sadly enough, because it's expected doesn't make it hurt any less. And make no mistake, betrayal has the potential to come from ANYONE. Parents, siblings, relatives and so-called friends. Be not dismayed, this battle is NOT ours (2 Chronicles 20:15). Now you've learned a lot by reading this book. The natural reaction is to want to find out who my egg donor is and beat her like she stole something. Trust me, I know the feeling well, but what I'm asking you as children of the Most High, is to pray for her. Don't get me wrong, I'm not defending her by any means, but I'm asking us (me included), to ask ourselves what is the correct way to handle the situation. That's not what this book is about. It's not about pointing fingers, getting back at anyone or trying to make anyone look a certain way. I'm also not trying to make myself look a certain way, I'm simply telling my story. It's a healing tool. A tool to help me in my healing process and to help someone else either continue to heal or get to their healing place. I want so much to never have another nightmare, to never feel un-protected or insecure. I want to let other VICTORS know they are not alone and that the abuse doesn't have to be the end. To help confirm for someone else that God is still an "on-time" God.

To let you see, through my experience that God is still in control and He's still in the blessing business. To help strengthen someone's faith so they will see that what they're going through isn't the end. It's not over until GOD says it's over. To help you understand that even someone as lowly as me has God on her side. So just like He came to my rescue, elevated me and brought me out, He's still doing the same thing and will do it for you. Just trust Him.

Like my Daddy said, "always do the right thing". We all have faults and even though her actions are trifling we have to pray for those who spitefully abuse us. Pray that the strong holds on her are broken. This experience has made me who I am. I'm a work in progress and I'm happy to wake up most mornings with a smile on my face. For what I've lost I've gained so much more. I have PHENOMENAL women in my life. I have women who see me as and love me like a daughter. I have women who are my sisters and love me just like I am. It is so wonderful having big sisters and little sisters and sisters to cry with and those who keep me in check and those that I love fighting with.

Ever heard the phrase "blood is thicker than water?" Well trust me it is so untrue. Not in all cases, but in a lot of them. Loyalty is my choice any day of the week. Blood, in my experience, will let you down most of the time. It's the loyalty from some family members and my true friends that have gotten me through the low patches in my life. Speaking of family, I'm sure there are some of them that will hate me for writing this. They will scandalize my name, ridicule me and drop me out of their lives like a hot potato just like before. It's not what I want, but I know it will happen. It's ok. I'm used to it and I will still pray for them.

I'm thankful for my parents who are excellent parents (all of you) and love me just for me and for my family and friends that love me just the same. For the ones that don't, "it is what it is".

I'm thankful for my former pastor and church family for letting me share my testimony. Pastor, several times you were talking to me when you were preaching and praying for me without even knowing it. Thank you for receiving me and my testimony and letting God get the glory from it.

I also want to thank my current church family for all of your support. God is elevating us for GREATER things.

Parents listen to, support and protect your children. They are gifts from God. And never forget that because a woman doesn't birth a child doesn't mean she's not a mother. There are a lot of women having babies that are not real mothers. None of us, especially me, are perfect. We have to look upward and know there is help there (Psalm 121). "I will lift mine eyes to the hills from whence cometh my help, my help cometh from the Lord." We will never be perfect, we just have to be willing to be good parents.

For those of you reading this with your own personal testimony, know that you are not alone. For the longest time I thought I was the only one to ever go through something like this. You are not alone. You are worthy of all that God has for you and I encourage you to look in the mirror and remind yourself of that. YOU CAN DO IT!

Ever notice a boll of cotton in a field? Its shell is hard, protective. Inside is a soft ball of cotton with seeds in it. Once it's processed the ball of cotton is so soft and ready to absorb and no seeds. That's me. That's us. That hard protective shell is God. He's keeping us, protecting us. The seeds are the things that are naturally in us, (hate, resentment, jealousy…) but things we need to get rid of so we can be used. Once God "processes us" i.e. we accept Him as our personal Savoir, we're then ready for use. Ponder that thought.

A wise man gave me 3 words when I discussed the book with him. PREPARATION. DEDICATION. CELEBRATION. Preparation- He told me the experience, the trials and tribulations I've gone through was God preparing me for this day. To use me as a tool to help someone else and allow God to get the glory from it when His people are delivered from the burdens they carry. Dedication- That's what it would take to see this book through to the end. There have been many rough patches just trying to get the words on paper. Celebration- that's what I'll do when it comes to pass and I'm not only holding the book in my hand, but it's helping people and God is truly getting the glory from it. Thank you Daddy! For those of you that every single time you see me feel it necessary to tell me how much I look like my egg-donor, please stop. It's not cute and it's nothing I want to hear. You've already said it hundreds of time, no need to keep repeating yourselves. I know there is no harm meant in your words, but it's something that I can live without. If I never hear it again it would be too soon. Please, I'm graciously asking, that you not say it anymore. At least not to me. Thank you for understanding.

I can't close this without thanking my SUPER-CALI-FRAGI-LISTIC-EXPI-ALI-DOCIOUS husband and daughter. They see me when I cry and smile. When I'm at my best and worst, my highs and lows and they still love me. Thank you for being so wonderful and for loving me. I couldn't make it without either of you.

Thank you to all my SHEROES that have gone through and survived! Your inspiration is priceless and means more than you know to me and so many others.

Still Standing

Thank you, reader, for going through this journey with me. I'm certain it was not an easy read, but you, like me, made it. When you pray, please include me and all the VICTORS in the world in your prayers. Little prayer, little power. Much prayer, much power. With much prayer we will continue to STAND!

Synopsis

In the depths of this book is the story of a young girl who finds herself, at a very young age, being sexually abused. She questions herself about what's happening to make sure she's not having a bad dream but the nightmare is real! She asks herself, "why am I going through this", "why is he doing this to me", "am I bad girl". He scares her into not telling with threats, but the time comes when she finally tells the one person she thought would be there for her, her mother, only to learn not only is she not believed, but her mother takes the abusers side. Now what? How will she make it through this situation? Will she succumb to what she feels like is a life of "sexual slavery" or will she find another way to fight?

Resources

If you are currently or have ever been a victim and want to become a VICTOR, please visit either

https://www.facebook.com/GreaterLifeCommunity?fref=ts   or www.nccasa.org.

Made in the USA
Columbia, SC
25 June 2024

37518079R00067